CAMBRIDGE MUSIC HANDBOOKS

Berg: Violin Concerto

CAMBRIDGE MUSIC HANDBOOKS

GENERAL EDITOR Julian Rushton

Cambridge Music Handbooks provide accessible introductions to major musical works, written by the most informed commentators in the field.

With the concert-goer, performer and student in mind, the books present essential information on the historical and musical context, the composition, and the performance and reception history of each work, or group of works, as well as critical discussion of the music.

Other published titles

Bach: Mass in B Minor JOHN BUTT
Handel: *Messiah* DONALD BURROWS
Haydn: *The Creation* NICHOLAS TEMPERLEY

Berg: Violin Concerto

Anthony Pople
Lancaster University

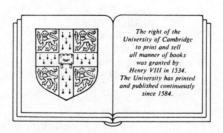

The right of the
University of Cambridge
to print and sell
all manner of books
was granted by
Henry VIII in 1534.
The University has printed
and published continuously
since 1584.

Cambridge University Press
Cambridge
New York   Port Chester
Melbourne   Sydney

Published by the Press Syndicate of the University of Cambridge
The Pitt Building, Trumpington Street, Cambridge CB2 1RP
40 West 20th Street, New York, NY 10011, USA
10 Stamford Road, Oakleigh, Melbourne 3166, Australia

First published 1991

Printed in Great Britain at the University Press, Cambridge

British Library cataloguing in publication data
Pople, Anthony, *1955*–
Berg: Violin Concerto. – (Cambridge music handbooks)
1. Austrian music. Berg, Alban, 1885–1935
I. Title
780.92

Library of Congress cataloguing in publication data
Pople, Anthony.
Berg, Violin Concerto / Anthony Pople.
p. cm. – (Cambridge music handbooks)
Includes bibliographical references and index.
ISBN 0 521 39066 4 – ISBN 0 521 39976 9 (pbk)
I. Berg, Alban 1885–1935. Concerto, violin, orchestra.
II. Title.
ML410.B47P6 1991
784.2'72–dc20 90–2542 CIP
72650
ISBN 0 521 39066 4 hardback
ISBN 0 521 39976 9 paperback

AJLP

for Lucy

Contents

Acknowledgements

It is a pleasure to record my debt to those who have helped in the preparation of this book. Eric Forder of Universal Edition, London, offered assistance during the early stages, as did Brian Kirtley, formerly Music Librarian at Lancaster University. I am especially grateful to Douglas Jarman, who gave generously both of his time and of his unrivalled specialist knowledge. The entire script was read in draft by Tim Carter, Douglas Jarman, Julian Rushton and Arnold Whittall; Karen Deering and Alain Frogley checked my translations from foreign-language sources. Their comments and advice were of immense value, though the responsibility for the text of the book remains mine alone.

I must also thank those who worked on behalf of Cambridge University Press to see this book into print: Margaret Jull Costa, my friendly and helpful copy-editor; Helen Beach, who dealt patiently with numerous enquiries about typography and layout; Lynn Hieatt, whose assistance and encouragement in practical matters was invaluable; and above all Penny Souster, who saw the whole thing through with characteristic efficiency. The book was typeset in the Music Department at Lancaster University, where colleagues and students bore the occasional neglect of my other duties with great understanding; members of my seminar on Extended Tonality will recognise parts of chapter 5, while Roger Bray's help with proof-reading was much appreciated. Last but by no means least, my thanks go to my wife and daughter, who supported me during the writing of the book and faithfully endured the preparation of camera-ready copy. To Lucy, who arrived at the same time as the contract and can now expect to see more of her father, the book is dedicated; I look forward to the day when she can read it.

The score and piano score of Berg's Violin Concerto are published by Universal Edition, Vienna; examples are reproduced by kind permission.

1

Musical ideologies: style and genre in the 1930s

In 1932, just three years before the composition of Berg's Violin Concerto, one of the most famous of all concerto recordings under a composer's baton was made in London. The young Yehudi Menuhin, then a teenage virtuoso, was perhaps the first and probably the last great violinist to make his recording debut with the work of a living composer. This was not the recent concerto by Stravinsky, however, nor the work of any other prominent composer of the age, but the concerto by Edward Elgar – then in his seventy-fifth year and no longer seriously active in his profession. In his lifetime, Elgar had participated in the growth of a thriving musical culture throughout Eastern and Western Europe, promoted by the growth of nationalism, but had more recently seen this culture all but destroyed in World War I. While the same nationalism was widely perceived as having sown the seeds of conflagration, the attention of nations was inevitably directed inwards during the period of rebuilding and reassessment which followed. The uncertainty thus engendered was to dictate changes in society which in turn affected musical life: the newly formed Soviet Union saw internal squabbles about the relation between progressive aesthetics and revolutionary politics; a xenophobic tendency latent in English musical nationalism now surfaced to the disadvantage of composers who maintained stylistic links with the European modernists. In addition, émigré composers became more numerous – many of them prominent names, such as Stravinsky, Rakhmaninov and Prokofiev; by the end of the 1930s the United States had become a refuge for the first and second of these, together with others such as Bartók, Britten, Hindemith, Weill and Arnold Schoenberg.

Schoenberg's musical thought was both a product and a definition of this uncertain age. By the 1930s his position in European musical life was established, yet the self-consciousness with which he charted and recharted his relationship to the German tradition was now perhaps even greater than in the early years of his career. Then, as a young composer doubly denied membership of a genuine oral tradition – both through being self-taught, and by virtue of the ideological split between broadly Brahmsian and broadly post-Wagnerian factions in German music – he had compensated for the first by throwing himself into composition teaching, and for the second by attempting to reconcile musical divisions through his own works. Post-Wagnerian harmonic and melodic writing was brought into conjunction with a Brahmsian approach to questions of form and genre in works such as the First Chamber Symphony, the First and Second String Quartets and the many songs he wrote at this time. By the early 1930s his attitudes had become more complex. In an essay written under the title 'National Music' in 1931, he acknowledged debts not only to Wagner and Brahms but also to Bach, Mozart and Beethoven.[1] The relationships which he claimed to the latter three compos-ers, however, were somewhat contrived; one might rather say that a new element had entered his musical ideology alongside the progressivism of Wagner and the classicised Romanticism of Brahms, in the shape of repeated allusion to unimpeachably great figures of the past: in writing by invoking them as precedents, and in music through elements of stylisation. And, in this most central of twentieth-century musical thinkers, a fourth strain of post-war ideology – simple conservatism – was ultimately asserted in works such as the Second Chamber Symphony and the Variations on a Recitative.

Allusion: Stravinsky and others

The new musical ideology of allusion was most fully explored by the French neoclassicists, and in particular by their émigré colleague, Stravinsky. As applied to his music, the term has come to have specific technical connotations, the most obvious to the listener being the play of pastiche and distortion within the ongoing texture of the music. This virtuoso stylistic serendipity is frequently underpinned by an allegiance to the octatonic scale of alternating semitones and whole tones, which allows familiar harmonic and linear configurations such as triads and modal tetrachords to be juxtaposed unusually but within a rational framework. At the same time, as Pieter van den Toorn has shown in his influential study of Stravinsky's music, the diatonic scale remains a point of reference, though its relation to the harmonic and melodic surface of the music is generally oblique – a characteristic which the great theorist Heinrich Schenker had already identified and disparaged in the 1920s.[2] But a more blindingly obvious contributing factor to Stravinsky's game of dislocation is his use of genre. The work which so aroused Schenker's wrath was the Concerto for piano and wind instruments;

2

other products of the 1920s and 1930s included the *Symphonies of Wind Instruments*, the *Symphony of Psalms* and the Concerto for two solo pianos, whose title-pages proclaim the indirectness of their relationships with established genres, which are thereby historically distanced. Even in the Octet for winds, the Sonata and the Serenade in A (both for piano), the Concerto in E♭ ('Dumbarton Oaks') and the Symphony in C – whose titles assert a straightforward relationship with their models – the generic assumptions aroused in the listener are as much toyed with as fulfilled.

Another such work is Stravinsky's own Concerto in D for violin and orchestra, which predates Berg's concerto by four years. Although not the wittiest of his neoclassical compositions, it raises and then evades expectations in numerous ways, not least by being cast in four movements rather than three. As Stravinsky himself pointed out to Robert Craft, the Bachian implications of the titles of these movements – Toccata, Aria I, Aria II and Capriccio – are only superficially followed through in the musical substance;[3] and though when composing the work he had told his publisher that he wanted to write 'a true virtuoso concerto',[4] the relationship of the finished concerto to this model was ambivalent:

... the texture is almost always more characteristic of chamber music than of orchestral music. I did not compose a cadenza, not because I did not care about exploiting the violin virtuosity, but because the violin in combination was my real interest. But virtuosity for its own sake has only a small role in my Concerto, and the technical demands of the piece are relatively tame.[5]

Others in France whose works at this time relied conspicuously on allusion were also using the concerto genre: Ravel's two Piano Concertos date from 1930 and 1931, Poulenc's *Concert Champêtre* (Rural Concerto) from 1928 and his two-piano Concerto in D minor from 1932. In other countries, Vaughan Williams (*Concerto Accademico*, 1925) and in a quite different way Kurt Weill (Concerto for violin and wind orchestra, 1924) wrote violin concertos which played on the listener's familiarity with Baroque music, while Hindemith – the most prominent modernist of his generation in Germany – made his name in the 1920s with a series of compositions entitled *Kammermusik* (Chamber Music), many of which, though not called concertos, were scored for soloist with orchestra or large ensemble. As this oblique relation to ready-made genres suggests, Hindemith was in many ways a more dedicated and sophisticated neoclassicist than the others mentioned above, Stravinsky always excepted: his thought embraced the social function of music as well as its structural aspect at all levels.

3

Conservatism: social and financial motivations

The use of allusion to historically distanced styles, in a lively game which constantly engages the listener's connoisseurship, must be distinguished from a straightforward allegiance to the genres and musical language of late Romanticism amounting merely to conservatism. Perhaps the best-known composer of the latter school was Rakhmaninov, whose Fourth Piano Concerto (1926), *Rhapsody on a Theme of Paganini* (1934), Third Symphony (1936) and Symphonic Dances (1940) are frequently spoken of and written about as if they were actually composed much earlier. It is more accurate – and more respectful to the composer – to regard this conservatism not as a throwback of some kind, but as a symptom of the age – an aesthetic position to which others were, or were to become, attracted. By the 1930s, Richard Strauss, whose stylistic development up to and including *Elektra* (1908) had made him one of the earliest composers to face the uncertainty of modernism, had long since opted for a conservative position. Younger composers came to it by a different route: Walton, for example, who had shone as a fashionable 'bright young thing' in the 1920s with *Façade* and *Portsmouth Point*, was by the mid-1930s writing to commission for the English musical Establishment. Oratorio, symphony and Coronation march featured in his output, and his association with figures active in right-wing politics probably also pushed him towards the conservatism that is the only musical ideology left visible in his Violin Concerto (1939).

In the United States, social and cultural conditions also tended to promote the genres of symphony and concerto as vehicles for conservatively late-Romantic music, for both had clear connotations of respectability in a country whose everyday language took the word 'symphony' to mean not only a piece of music but also the body of musicians who played it – and even the building in which it was played. The success of *Rhapsody in Blue* (1924) was nurtured by the self-professed cultural bridge-building of Paul Whiteman's 'symphonic' jazz; Gershwin's Piano Concerto (1925) and his subsequent concert works appealed to the same taste. No less clearly than Stravinsky's, these pieces show how the use of certain genres could itself amount to a statement – in this case, of a desire to belong; indeed, the link with Stravinsky is stronger than coincidence, since so many of the Russian composer's works at this time – the Serenade, *Apollo*, the *Symphony of Psalms*, the Violin Concerto, *Jeu de Cartes*, the 'Dumbarton Oaks' Concerto and the Symphony in C – were written to American commissions.[6] When commerce and a desire for social respectability played such a large part in forming the cultural environment,

4

it was perhaps hardly surprising that commissioning agents should tend towards the maintenance of established norms. This doubtless coincided fully with the aesthetic inclinations of some composers, such as the US-exiled Rakhmaninov, but it was the performing musician who was closest to the business side of music, and the most likely to have his tastes shaped by its constraints. The careers of most virtuosi – and not only in America – were centred on their performances of Romantic concertos, and it was Rakhmaninov the virtuoso pianist who, in effect, commissioned a fourth concerto and the *Rhapsody on a Theme of Paganini* from Rakhmaninov the composer. Other composer–pianists, such as Gershwin, could follow this time-honoured practice, just as a composer–conductor might, if he so wished, write a symphony for his own baton. When, on the other hand, the commission came from a virtuoso of another instrument – as with Louis Krasner's approach to Berg – the extent to which the cultural conditions supporting the commission might be transmitted to the composer's sensibility was less pre-determined. Berg did not know Krasner well and may not have appreciated that he had a serious interest in the music of the Schoenberg school; his motivation was far from being solely or even largely commercial. But then neither was his career as a virtuoso ultimately successful.

It was also Schoenberg's American period which saw the emergence of a conservative strain in his music, not only in the plainly tonal works such as the Suite in G and the Theme and Variations for band – the latter composed at his publisher's behest, i.e. for commercial reasons – but also more generally, in a preoccupation with some of the questions of musical form which had occupied him in the first decade of the century. This conservatism was not specifically linked with the use of established genres, although one should observe that his only two concertos date from the American years – the Violin Concerto from 1936 and the Piano Concerto from 1942 – in addition to a four-movement symphony which was substantially sketched in 1937.[7] On the contrary, perhaps the most characteristic aspect of Schoenberg's relation to the various musical ideologies outlined here was his capacity for balance, or even synthesis, which had been signalled at the outset of his career by his apparent efforts to follow simultaneously the progressivist and classicising strands of thought then evident in German music. Schoenberg was, of course, not the only composer who exhibited this kind of mastery. To look no further than the violin concertos of the 1930s, one can see how, in their respective second concertos for the instrument, Prokofiev (1935), Szymanowski (1935) and Bartók (1938) achieved artistic success through a balanced approach which paid more than mere respect to the Romantic connotations of the genre

5

without at the same time entirely abandoning the highly personal styles they had forged under the successive banners of modernism and nationalism. Similarly, in the works he composed during the 1920s and 1930s, Schoenberg's most prominent pupil beside Berg, Anton Webern, encapsulated the expressionist language of his earlier works within the boundaries of a coolly controlled technical means, while making allusive use of classical forms and genres.

Berg: synthesis or symbiosis?

Berg was arguably more adept even than Schoenberg in his achievement of such balance between deeply contrasting elements. Indeed, Stravinsky went so far as to describe Berg's music as 'synthetic (in the best sense)', meaning presumably that it embodies a synthesis of ideas without appearing to be 'manufactured', though he gave no indication in musical terms of how he felt this was achieved.[8] A comparison with Schoenberg suggests that Berg's ability to reflect different ideological positions in the different elements of his music was more subtle, less coarse-grained, than that of his master. As has been noted above, a number of Schoenberg's early compositions match a progressivist melodic and harmonic language with a broadly classicist approach to generic expectations and formal structure. In the 1920s, the serial method, by a stroke of genius, allowed him genuinely to synthesise this classically conceived technique with its post-tonal, progressive musical consequences for melody and harmony. But his allusive use of formats such as Suite, Serenade, Variations and Wind Quintet in the 1920s was on a different plane; to this extent, Schoenberg laid himself open to the kind of criticism which Brahms had suffered, namely that he was wilfully separating form and content. According to this view, Schoenberg's greatest compositions came from a period in which, like Stravinsky in the inter-war years, he gave virtually free rein to but a single ideology – the 'expressionist' works of 1908–16, such as *Erwartung* and the Five Orchestral Pieces, in which generic and formal norms were set aside, leaving the progressive orientation richly in control of all musical elements.

It was precisely this sort of writing which Berg abandoned, at Schoenberg's insistence, when he composed the Three Orchestral Pieces. But the techniques he had learned in his early years were not forgotten. Indeed, his compositions from this time on were to build on each other with a remarkable consistency, successively bringing in new musical ideas and approaches which, though readily visible on their first appearance, would subsequently be absorbed into the characteristic Bergian symbiosis. For example, the stylisation of form has a high profile in *Wozzeck*; it is also to be found in the works which followed, but merely as one aspect of a more complex attitude to formal organisation. Whereas in most of Schoenberg's compositions, and in those of many lesser composers, different ideologies each inform different elements of the music, in the works of Berg's maturity each musical element is simultaneously informed by several different ideologies. The result is not genuinely a synthesis, but gives the illusion of one – just as a mosaic or a pointillist painting may communicate a coherent image from a fine-grained approximation. Conservatism of a sort is evident as early as the Three Orchestral Pieces, but becomes continuously audible for the first time as an underlying factor in the melodic and harmonic writing of *Der Wein* – albeit melded with a large element of stylistic allusion. Its role in the Violin Concerto is undoubtedly fuller, however, and has provoked criticism. As suggested above, it could perhaps be 'accounted for' as a consequence of the circumstances of the work's commission; at the same time, the literature of music appreciation indicates that it has helped to make the concerto more accessible than any other piece of serial music.

The concerto as model

While this discussion has been overtly concerned with a particular genre, it has indicated that the use of certain generic models in the 1920s and 1930s amounted in itself to an ideological statement in music. These therefore cannot be regarded as abstract categories transparent to the gaze of historical criticism: to divide the music of this period genre by genre is to obscure a vital element of musical thought. The history of the nineteenth-century symphony, opera or concerto is generally coherent, and sometimes remains so even when geographical divisions are additionally applied; the post-1920 concerto, on the other hand, is a strange beast, as a comparison among the works mentioned in the foregoing pages will confirm. And since the essence of genre lies in the relation of specific instances to larger categories, this means that the concept itself was brought into question through such usage.

In a broader sense also, this was the age of the individual – a fact merely confirmed by the protestations of self-conscious groupings such as Les Six and the Schoenberg school. Ironically, it was precisely the relation of the individual to the undifferentiated mass which, in the Romantic model established by Paganini, Liszt and others, was the essential dialectic of the concerto genre itself, to be pursued through the interaction between soloist and orchestra. Rakhmaninov's works testified to the survival of an ideal in which the individual is triumphant; on the other hand, Stravinsky's comments on his own Violin Concerto (see p. 3), and the concerto grosso framework that he and others revived during this period, suggested a relationship between equals that was to gain its clearest such expression in Bartók's Concerto for Orchestra (1943). Berg's work characteristically explored the space between these alternatives: in the relationship between soloist and orchestra the work has many hallmarks of a Romantic concerto. At the same time, the manner in which the soloist leads the orchestral strings towards the climax of its last movement points strongly in the other direction. Critical assessment of the work has frequently taken up the further question of how this dialectic between confrontation and reconciliation is transposed to the musical substance itself through the interaction between tonal stylistic references and the serial idiom, and whether it is satisfactorily resolved. Unfortunately, such written discussion cannot expect similarly to synthesise a consideration of individual and generic characteristics, but must move strategically from the general to the particular or vice versa. The format of this book allows for the music of Berg's concerto to be brought gradually into the close focus of an analytical investigation, and then conversely for the results of this to re-emerge into the larger context of critical evaluation.

2

Towards the Violin Concerto

After the completion of the *Lyric Suite* on 26 September 1926, Berg composed only three more works: the concert aria *Der Wein*, the opera *Lulu* and the Violin Concerto.[1] Clearly, the two shorter works are literally dwarfed by the opera, which is of three hours' duration – about as long as all his other works put together, *Wozzeck* excepted. But the aria and the concerto lie within the orbit of *Lulu* in a way more directly relevant to their musical characteristics, in that the former was not begun until work on the opera was well under way, while the latter was completed with work on the opera still unfinished: both were, in effect, interruptions of the larger project. The early chronology of the *Lulu* years also included the preparation of an orchestral version of the *Seven Early Songs* (1905–8) and a revision of the Three Orchestral Pieces (1914–15), thus bringing Berg into direct working contact with his pre-war music at a time when he was forging a sound-world and a musical language for his masterpiece and its satellites. Commentators from Stravinsky to George Perle have identified the Three Orchestral Pieces as in many ways representing the beginning of Berg's maturity: from this point on, a number of recurrent or developing technical features are clearly in evidence from one work to the next. But the small size of Berg's total output makes the individuality of each work the more striking, and the chronological spread of the mature works is generous, covering twenty dramatic years in Western music. In comparing works from 1915 and 1935, even by a single highly individual composer, one cannot possibly imagine that one is comparing like with like: the identification of stylistic and technical fingerprints among these compositions must to a certain extent remain schematic, but should be understood within a complex historical perspective.

When he began work on the Three Orchestral Pieces, Berg already had behind him a large quantity of essentially Romantic songs, together with a Piano Sonata (Op. 1, 1907–8), a String Quartet (Op. 3, 1910) and two works – the *Altenberg Lieder* (Op. 4, 1912) and the Four Pieces for clarinet and piano (Op. 5, 1913) – in which he had gone some way towards exploring the

9

aphoristic style of which Webern was to become the master. As is well known, the composition of the orchestral pieces followed a confrontation of sorts with Schoenberg over these miniatures.[2] Berg's next work was bound to be reactionary to some extent, therefore, and a letter to Schoenberg from the summer of 1913 indicates the terms of reference against which this reaction was formed:

. . . Unfortunately I have to confess, dear Herr Schönberg, that I haven't made use of your various suggestions as to what I should compose next. Much as I was intrigued from the start by your suggestion to write an orchestral suite (with character pieces), and though I immediately began to think of it often and seriously . . . nonetheless it didn't come about. Again and again I found myself giving in to an older desire – namely to write a symphony. And when I intended to make a concession to this desire by beginning the suite with a prelude, I found . . . that it again turned merely into the opening of this symphony. So I simply decided to go ahead with it: – it is to be a large one-movement symphony . . . [similar] in construction to [your] Chamber Symphony. Concurrently though, the plan for the suite is sure to mature to the point where I can actually begin writing it, and then your kind suggestion will be realized – though belatedly. I hope with all my heart that you won't be angry with me for postponing realization of your suggestion . . . If during these last months I have thought so often and intensely about writing a symphony it is surely because . . . I want to heed your words, 'Each of your students should at some point have written a symphony.'[3]

The first thing to note, perhaps, is that Berg never did write a symphony – though it was among the projects he had it in mind to pursue after orchestrating *Lulu*.[4] Nor do the Three Orchestral Pieces constitute a suite in the sense Schoenberg seems to have intended. But the composer was later to describe the five scenes which make up Act I of *Wozzeck* as character pieces, the first of which is laid out as a suite using Baroque dance forms, and was to characterise the five scenes of Act II as 'inseparably linked together as the movements of a (in this case, dramatic) symphony'.[5] In fact, the dialectic of genre between symphony and suite retained its importance in the composer's mind to the end, as is shown by the double plan for both a *Lulu Symphony* and a *Lulu Suite* which he proposed to his publisher in 1934.[6] The solution in this case was the publication of the five movements intended for the suite under the title *Symphonische Stücke* (Symphonic Pieces).

From the Three Orchestral Pieces to the *Lyric Suite*

Even in 1913, such a fusion of half-evaded formal and generic expectations, as an alternative to the evident straightforwardness of Schoenberg's advice, was already characteristic of Berg. His early Piano Sonata and String Quartet

(Opp. 1 and 3) are ostensibly cast in genres whose classicist credentials had been thoroughly established by Brahms and other like-minded composers before the turn of the century, but their closer relationship to these schemata is idiosyncratic. The Sonata consists of a single movement – though it was planned in three – and the String Quartet has but two. Many features of the Piano Sonata, not least its exposition repeat, point to a Brahmsian conception of the genre having been compromised by the decision to allow the single movement to stand alone. But if this compromise may be seen as akin to, say, the general acceptance among musicians that Schubert's unfinished B minor symphony is a viable whole – admittedly more by accident than design – then the departure of Berg's String Quartet from the model invoked on its title-page is more determinedly radical. Whereas Schoenberg's First and Second String Quartets (1904–5, 1907–8) tackle the classicist legacy of the genre head-on through their approach to musical form and the interrelationship of movements, Berg's work hardly acknowledges these things. Even if one accepts Hans Redlich's view that in the relationship between its two thematically related slow movements the quartet bears comparison with the later symphonies of Mahler, in which previously classicised large- and small-scale formal models are re-Romanticised to remarkable effect,[7] this must be seen as an early and genuine influence, rather than a precocious example of the linguistic symbiosis of Berg's maturity.

As his career proceeded, Berg's thought showed an increasing quality of deliberation, which doubtless stemmed from the deep personal reassessment prompted by Schoenberg's harsh words. Research of all kinds since his death has demonstrated that his statements and lecture on *Wozzeck*, his open letter to Schoenberg on facets of the Chamber Concerto and the analysis of *Lulu* which he communicated via his pupil and biographer Willi Reich merely hint at a sophistry which was kept hidden from even his closest colleagues. The manifold accommodations and symbioses within the musical language of the Three Orchestral Pieces were the first evidence of this complexity. While the music is essentially thematic, as Stravinsky later pointed out,[8] each piece, the first especially so, emerges out of a texture in which motivic and thematic material is deployed with the sparse clarity of the *Altenberg Lieder* and the pieces for clarinet and piano. But if this characteristic aligns Berg's Op. 6 with the sets of orchestral pieces composed at around the same time by Schoenberg and Webern, the length of the pieces and their clear formal outlines make even this generic association an ambivalent one. Rather, as Perle has suggested, the elaborate technique of thematic working, which forges interrelationships among the pieces and so lends a sense of integration to the entire set, 'is

11

indebted to the pre-atonal works of Schoenberg'.[9] In this sense, the work shows a trait of conservatism which was then new to Berg's music, but was to remain with him and would emerge in a number of ways in his later works.

Whatever Berg's debt to Schoenberg in these pieces, however, their most far-reaching link is with the sound-world and rhetoric of Mahler. To Adorno, this marked, paradoxically, a crucial advance for the Second Viennese School:

The new breadth [is shown in] . . . the work's stylistic range. Berg's insistent working out of his own specific methods brings him, without sacrificing a single one of Schoenberg's discoveries, into a material relationship with music beyond the Schoenberg circle: that of Mahler and Debussy. With the Orchestral Pieces, the Schoenberg school moves directly and purposefully into the stylistic movement of its time, or rather reveals itself as the style-defining instantiation of that movement, a position which in truth it had held since its evolution: not an esoteric sect with a private idiom and a conspiratorial way of thinking, but a progressive agent for the fulfilment of musical understanding, thinking through what was only dimly inherent in the developing forces of contemporary composition . . . Berg has, it seems, shown the backward line linking the Schoenbergian musical language with what had gone before, and secured the resulting advance through contact with the past. But the backward line was itself extended, in consequence of its own development, towards the future. Never in the ideological sense of the new classicists, who pass off the old, rehashed, as new . . . but rather through the obligation that proceeds from a distinctly different response to the great call to order, which in the Orchestral Pieces establishes the similarity with Debussy and Mahler . . . This explains why Berg's most Mahler-like, most painterly [*Mahlerischste*] score is the most complicated he ever wrote. With chords of many notes and the clashing counterpoint of countless simultaneous voices, he surpassed in a wild frenzy that which in modern music previously had arisen merely as goodly provocation.[10]

But Adorno's concern to portray Berg as unambiguously progressive, and his over-emotional reaction to the neoclassical movement, make his picture of the composer disappointingly one-sided. Despite his identification of a broad stylistic range as one of the crucial hallmarks of this work, he is inclined to undervalue its most audible Mahlerian characteristic, namely the element of allusion. For the Three Orchestral Pieces are Mahlerian not only in the quality of their sound-world and emotional climate, but also in their use of march and waltz materials to extend the range of musical gesture by allusion to the banal – something which Adorno found distasteful. It is probably this feature, though, which prompted Perle to suggest that the Mahlerian traits established in his Op. 6 were to remain with Berg to the end of his life, and that 'in both *Lulu* and the Violin Concerto . . . there are episodes that still show the strong influence of Mahler, and that still stand close to the Three Pieces'.[11]

12

Certainly, the use of lowbrow musical *objets trouvés* within a complex play of generic models is a conspicuous device in every major work of Berg's after the Three Orchestral Pieces, with the exception only of the *Lyric Suite*. In *Wozzeck*, there is Andres's folk song (Act I scene 2), the military march (I.3), the waltz music accompanying the Doctor's diagnoses (I.4 and II.2), a whole variety of things in the tavern scene (II.4), the honky-tonk polka (III.3) and the children's nursery rhyme (III.5). The Chamber Concerto also has a good deal of waltz music; *Der Wein* and *Lulu*, on the other hand, have jazz; in addition, the opera's third act revolves around variations on a cabaret song and its score includes orchestral imitations of a mouth-organ, a mechanical circus-organ and a street barrel-organ. The use of a Carinthian folk tune in the Violin Concerto is musically akin to these examples – remembering always that, like each of them, it has a meaning of its own deriving from its context in the poetry of the work as a whole.

At the same time, there are examples of stylistic allusion which are not so blatantly placed within quotation marks, as it were. Marie's lullaby in Act I scene 3 of *Wozzeck* is one such instance: it might be called an affectionate parody, were the element of parody not so completely mollified by the quality of the affection. Stravinsky's self-diagnosed 'rare form of kleptomania',[12] by which he appropriated for his own purposes the music he loved, was mild by comparison with Berg's ability to distil tiny elements of style and technique from music of all kinds and to reconstitute them in a way which melded them together, yet which also preserved sufficient differentiation for the music's multiple allusions to be heard by the listener. This is particularly clear towards the end of his career: *Lulu* is littered with subtle examples of momentary allusion, and shot through with music which from moment to moment suggests something else – but not so clearly that one can point exactly to what that something else is. The Chamber Concerto and the *Lyric Suite* are transitional in this sense: the bar-by-bar musical language of the concerto points towards the later symbiosis but lacks the glittering surface which might cue the range of styles within it; the music of the *Lyric Suite* is even more 'of a piece', including nothing which can really be called an allusion, but it does quote literally, if briefly, from Zemlinsky's *Lyric Symphony* and Wagner's *Tristan und Isolde*.

The impact of serial technique

The transitional nature of these works – and of the 1925 setting of Theodor Storm's 'Schliesse mir die Augen beide' – is undoubtedly a consequence of

Berg's initial difficulty in integrating the new technique of serial composition into his magpie nest. Serial technique itself did not define a musical language – that is, it did not fully specify the kinds of harmony which were to be written, nor their progression, nor the ways in which melodic lines were to move among pitches; at least not in a way which went beyond the elementary shapes set down in the series itself. Each work was to have its own series of twelve notes to which all pitches in the music were related: at each moment, every sounding pitch would be a member of some version of the series – possibly derived from the original by transposition and mirror inversion – which was but briefly before the ear. Thus the compositional process involved creating diversity out of a stringent unity. How, on the other hand, was one work to sound like the next? How was the larger musical language to be reunified, when each work had its own distinct series? Serial principles did not answer these questions. Nevertheless, the works which Schoenberg, Berg and Webern wrote using the technique confirm that each had his own style: the music of all three sounds different because the compositions of each sound similar. When it was difficult to forge even one style, however, Berg's penchant for parody and allusion, far from giving him a natural advantage, made his position yet more difficult. His quotation of the opening of *Tristan* in the last movement of the *Lyric Suite* was actually a remarkable triumph in this respect, as Erwin Stein noted at the time.[13] The accommodation of an almost diatonic cabaret song into the serial texture of *Lulu*, and the Lutheran chorale melody 'Es ist genug' into the Violin Concerto, represented a further masterly development along these lines.

In part, the distinction between the music of the three composers of the Schoenberg circle derives from their different ways with matters of rhythm and orchestration, and indeed musical texture generally. Berg's most characteristic rhythmic device – the rhythmic motive, or *Hauptrhythmus*, which is such a notable feature of *Lulu* and the Violin Concerto – is presaged as early as the *Altenberg Lieder* and in the Mahlerian fate rhythms of the Three Orchestral Pieces,[14] but it is codified for the first time in Act III scene 3 of *Wozzeck*. Here the obsessive use of a single rhythm (though with variety gained through its appearance at different speeds, and in continual counterpoint with itself) wonderfully expresses Wozzeck's blundering efforts to act normally while his mind is inescapably full of the murder he has just committed. That the *Hauptrhythmus* of the Chamber Concerto also arose from a poetic intent was made clear in Berg's open letter to Schoenberg, though the details of the work's 'world of human–emotional associations' have only recently been revealed through the sketch studies of Brenda Dalen.[15] These

Example 1. *Hauptrhythmen* of (a) *Lyric Suite*; (b), (c) *Lulu*; (d) Violin Concerto

precedents for the rhythmic motives used dramatically in *Lulu* and the Violin
Concerto helped to maintain a continuity of practice between Berg's serial
works and those which preceded them.

Indeed, the introduction of the series into Berg's compositional palette was
not divorced from his rhythmic techniques. On the contrary, he developed
a specific method of linking the establishment of motivic patterns within the
twelve-note totality to the adoption of a rhythmic pattern as a *Hauptrhythmus*,
as he explained in a letter to Schoenberg.[16] From the musical realisation of
this idea in the *Allegro misterioso* movement of the *Lyric Suite*, it is clear that
the crucial contextual factor is the ostinato-like statement of the twelve-note
series in a texture of undifferentiated note-values – here regular semiquavers
– against which the characteristic rhythm is plainly established. By this means,
the process of partitioning the series into a seven-note chromatic scale and
complementary five-note melodic motive (Example 1a) results simultaneously
in the generation of what Berg called a 'characteristic rhythm' and its
complement. In later works, however, he gradually dispensed with this
strictness. Although the *Hauptrhythmus* of *Lulu* also originated in the
derivation of subsidiary material from the main series of the opera – in this
case the sinuous chromatics associated with the character of Schigolch
(Example 1b) – Berg freely adapted the rhythm to the form in which it
pervades the most fatalistic passages of the work (Example 1c) when he
returned to the opera after composing *Der Wein*, a work which itself has no
Hauptrhythmus. The fate-laden programme of the Violin Concerto evidently
demanded the use of a *Hauptrhythmus* (Example 1d); but the specific rhythm
Berg used – which is remarkably close to that found in the third movement

of the *Lyric Suite* – is not connected with any schematic partitioning of the series.[17]

As his letter to Schoenberg about the *Lyric Suite* demonstrates, the patchwork constructivism promoted by the close focus of the twelve-note series was one aspect of the new technique which was admirably suited to Berg's sensibility. Adorno's epithet, 'the Master of the smallest transition', is apt in its indication of the composer's miraculous ability to produce coherent music from tiny fragments. The rich cross-references within the music of *Lulu*, for example, include many minute details which are essentially anecdotal in nature. But Berg's ability to knit disparate musical objects together extended also through broader, more perceptible transitions – such as the passages which link the two major sections of each movement of the Violin Concerto – to the largest levels of musical organisation. The major cross-references which consolidate the formal structure of *Lulu* – making the work, in Perle's view, simultaneously a 'number opera' and a through-composed music drama[18] – are on a completely different scale, involving the repetition, variation and recapitulation of whole sections of music.

At this level, the constructivism so characteristic of serial music interacted with Berg's allusive use of stylised forms such as sonata and rondo, which began in *Wozzeck*. The composer himself, notably in his 1929 lecture on the opera, described how the fifteen scenes, together with the final interlude, are each distinguished by an individual design.[19] Many of these are reinterpretations of older archetypes: in this sense, Act I 'includes' a Suite, a Rhapsody, a Military March and Lullaby, a Passacaglia and a Rondo; Act II is supposedly a five-movement symphony, with a sonata movement, a Fantasia and Fugue, a *Largo* slow movement, a Scherzo and a Rondo finale; the music of Act III comprises six 'inventions'. Thus the stylistic *objets trouvés* of the Three Orchestral Pieces are joined by formal *objets* from an earlier age. In line with Adorno's characterisation of Berg's Op. 6, Joseph Kerman has suggested that the opera is closer to the repertoire operas of Strauss and Puccini than is Schoenberg's *Erwartung*, yet by comparison with the latter work derives its strength from that very normality.[20]

Remarkably, it was also through these textbook forms that Berg first began to reach an accommodation with Schoenberg's serial principles, in the first movement of the Chamber Concerto. The movement is cast in the form of a theme and five variations, but only the first and last variations proceed by the traditional principle of decoration and textural elaboration of the theme. On the contrary, the intervening variations are related to the theme – all thirty bars of it – as retrograde, inversion and inverted retrograde: in each case, the entire pitch-structure is turned through 180 degrees and recast in a way which makes musical sense. But this 'musical sense' is still pursued through the post-Romantic gestures which surface so effectively in the Three Orchestral Pieces and *Wozzeck*. Berg's first approach to serialism was not at the nuts-and-bolts level for which Schoenberg conceived the technique.

The audible and the inaudible

Paradoxically, this apparently more sophisticatedly musical line of thought opened up a division between the audible and inaudible dimensions of Berg's work. The mirror-related variations in the Chamber Concerto are already barely audible as such, but beyond this, the work incorporates musical ciphers and numerological patterns which cannot possibly be heard. Nor can they have been intended to be heard; nor, indeed, can one say – as some have said of the Golden Section proportions occasionally found in the music of Debussy and Bartók – that the patterns have a natural, organic quality which allows them somehow to be felt, even if they are not directly perceived. The Chamber Concerto has a double life: its musical organisation is shadowed by a web of intriguing and fantastic concepts, incorporating themes based in a manner akin to the famous B–A–C–H motto on the names of Arnold Schoenberg (A–D–S–C–H–B–E–G), Anton von Webern (A–E–B–E) and Alban Berg (A–B–E–G), together with an obsessive use of the number three and its multiples for the lengths of both shorter and longer sections of the music, as measured by the number of bars in the score. Even the metronome markings at each change of tempo are divisible by three. Later works continued this trend, but with a richer musical language, rendering their symbioses of the audible and the inaudible yet more remarkable. In the words of Douglas Jarman, 'it is this apparently paradoxical fusion of technical calculation and emotional spontaneity that gives Berg's music its peculiar fascination'.[21]

It is clear that Berg was fascinated by numerological and geometrical schemes of all kinds, but particularly with those which could in some way be applied to music. The second movement of the Chamber Concerto, 240 bars in length, is the earliest example of a virtually precise large-scale palindrome in his music. The outer sections of the *Allegro misterioso* of the *Lyric Suite* present the same music 'forwards' and then 'backwards', and the central section of *Der Wein* is a palindrome within itself. But in each of these examples there is an evident compromise both with the left-to-right orientation of aural perception and with the classical ternary form (ABA) which, operating within these perceptual confines, had for several centuries approximated the

17

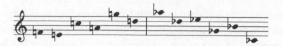

Example 2. *Lyric Suite*: series of first movement

palindrome in music. In the *Allegro misterioso*, while the two A sections of the ABA layout are related as prime and retrograde, the B section (the *Trio estatico*) is through-composed. In *Der Wein*, the opposite arrangement applies: the A sections are through-composed while the B section is palindromic. Moreover, the retrograde part of the palindrome in each case is abbreviated, in line with its musical function as a reprise of earlier material – a function which, as the second A section in *Der Wein* illustrates, does not depend for its effectiveness on the complete restatement of the recapitulated material.

Although the appearance of palindromic forms in Berg's later works clearly relates to the serial concept of prime and retrograde orientations, it also has resonances well beyond the Schoenberg circle: to the palindromic forms developed shortly afterwards by Bartók, for example, and as one precedent for the more complex patterns that were later to be employed by Messiaen. In a similarly unexpected way, the resurgence of tonality in these works through the aurally allusive appearance of the basic building blocks of tonal music – chords and scales – arose in the context of intricate twelve-note serial working. The series on which both his 1925 setting of 'Schliesse mir die Augen beide' and the first movement of the *Lyric Suite* are based (Example 2) is an all-interval series; that is to say, not only is each of the twelve notes of the octave represented once and once only – as is of course to be expected – but the series also contains a single instance of each of the possible intervals, from a minor second (one semitone) to a major seventh (eleven semitones), between its adjacent notes. But perhaps the most striking property of this geometrically precise series is that it also falls cleanly into two halves along tonal lines: the first six notes lie within the scale of F major (or that of C major), while the last six lie within the scale of B major (or F$^\sharp$) – though Berg notated them enharmonically in C$_\flat$ major when describing the series to Schoenberg.[22]

The discovery in 1977 of a secret programme for the *Lyric Suite* revealed that this purely musical paradox was only the tip of a remarkable iceberg.[23] Dedicating the work privately to Hanna Fuchs-Robettin, the wife of a Prague industrialist, Berg enshrined their four initials (A–B, H–F) in a four-note motive, used the numbers 10 (for Hanna) and 23 (for himself) as the basis for the lengths of sections of the work and for its metronome markings (as with the number three in the Chamber Concerto), and provided Hanna with an annotated score showing how tiny details in the music were to be construed as references to her and to the course of their (almost certainly unconsummated) relationship. Most remarkably of all, he showed how the last movement of this work for string quartet alone was in fact a setting of a text by Baudelaire (in German translation), in which the quartet was apparently to be joined by a mezzo-soprano. Here was truly a piece with a double life. After this discovery it became possible to entertain the idea that other writings and compositions of Berg's dating from the mid-1920s and after might contain ciphers and numerical references to Hanna Fuchs. Thus Berg's explicit reference to the tonalities of F and H (the German letter-name for B♮) in his description to Schoenberg of the *Lyric Suite* series – despite the alternative tonal allegiances of C and F♯, and despite the enharmonic respelling of C♭ major as B major which was entailed – suggests an extraordinary convergence of the most arcane of private references with that feature of his serial works which was to do the most for their accessibility: the highly audible inclusion of musical configurations normally associated with tonality.[24]

A second opera

As the *Lyric Suite* neared completion, Berg began to cast around for a subject for his second opera. His search proceeded slowly: in January 1927 he wrote jokingly to Schoenberg that 'there's not much chance of an opera at the moment, much as every play entices me to compose it'.[25] By the end of November, however, he had narrowed his choice down to a setting of either Gerhart Hauptmann's *Und Pippa tanzt!* or the *Lulu* tragedies of Frank Wedekind. Unable to decide between these alternatives, he sought the advice of Theodor Adorno, who tried to persuade him in favour of the Wedekind,[26] but within two months he had settled instead on *Pippa*, taking Webern and Schoenberg into his confidence at the beginning of 1928.[27] As a house guest of Alma Mahler Werfel towards the end of January he met Hauptmann personally for the first time and discussed the project with him,[28] and by the end of March he was making plans for the libretto.[29] But *Pippa* was dogged from the start by contractual difficulties with Hauptmann's publishers, who insisted on exorbitant royalties. Within a month Berg was confessing to serious doubts,[30] and by the end of June he was working after all on the Wedekind.[31]

In the meantime, he had completed an orchestral version of seven of the ninety or so songs which date from his earliest years (1905–8).[32] Whether or not the songs were substantially revised for publication, there is no doubt that

Berg's renewed contact with their idiom at this time should not be overlooked in discussing the characteristic style of his last works. Perle has likened the musical language of the *Seven Early Songs* to that of Schoenberg's *Gurrelieder*, a work to which Berg had written a lengthy introductory guide, as well as preparing the vocal score – a vast undertaking over which he took immense pains.[33] In Perle's view, the formal structure of the *Gurrelieder* set a precedent for the design of both *Wozzeck* and *Lulu*, with its 'integration within a large-scale design of self-contained individual numbers that remain clearly differentiated in spite of thematic and harmonic interrelations'.[34] At a more fundamental level, it is to the post-Wagnerian harmonic vocabulary and syntax exemplified by the *Gurrelieder* that one should look in identifying aspects of tonality in the music of the *Lulu* period, rather than to the technicalities of far earlier styles which form the substance of received ideas on tonal theory. That Berg knew this music inside out is borne out by his guides not only to the *Gurrelieder* but also to Schoenberg's *Pelleas und Melisande* and First Chamber Symphony. Moreover, his preparation of the index to Schoenberg's *Harmonielehre* (1911) must have lent schematic clarification to his no doubt instinctive technical appreciation of the harmonic language of these works. The *Seven Early Songs*, though composed in their original form several years before his work on the *Gurrelieder*, show a similar command of late-Romantic tonal harmony, together with the modernistic resources described in the later chapters of the *Harmonielehre*, such as the whole-tone scale and chords constructed in fourths. Moreover, both in their subtle contours and in their tendency to dominate the musical texture, the melodic lines of these songs are directly comparable to the vocal lines of *Der Wein* and *Lulu* and the solo part of the Violin Concerto.

In contrast to the frustrations of *Pippa*, work on *Lulu* at first went well, and within a few months Berg was able to tell Schoenberg that over 300 bars had already been composed.[35] But his work was soon interrupted by other chores and then by the necessity of a return to Vienna from the temporary peace of the Berg family estate – the 'Berghof' – in Carinthia. (His way of life in the capital, and the visits he necessarily made to other cities in connection with performances of his works, generally left little time for composition.) Early in 1929 he prepared his lecture on *Wozzeck*, and by early May he had made revisions to the score of the Three Orchestral Pieces in preparation for their premiere in Oldenburg, which was to take place the following year.[36] Then came a commission from the soprano Ruzena Herlinger for a concert aria. The fee of 5,000 schillings made this an attractive project, and so the first part of

Example 3. *Der Wein*: (a) series, prime form; (b) inversion (notes 7–12)

his summer period in Carinthia, from the end of May to mid-August, was devoted to it.[37] Another month's work on *Lulu* followed; but in contrast to his good rate of progress the previous year he now found work on the opera very difficult, as he confessed to Webern on 20 September.[38] By the end of the month he had left the Berghof for Vienna, and had left the composition of *Lulu* at approximately bar 521 of Act I scene 2 – just before the entrance of Dr Schön.[39]

For the text of *Der Wein* (*Wine*), Berg turned again to the translation by Stefan George of Baudelaire's *Les Fleurs du mal*, from which he had already taken the text for the secret vocal finale of the *Lyric Suite*.[40] In consideration of the excellent cellars of Hanna Fuchs-Robettin's husband, it is probably reasonable to infer a reference to her in the aria's subject matter – though clearly less weighty in tone than the private references of the *Lyric Suite*. The work is also far less constructivist in organisation than the quartet, the palindromic layout of the central section excepted. Indeed, at the smaller level of note-by-note working, the musical language is undoubtedly more inclined towards the accessible, and even the vernacular, than in any previous work of Berg's maturity, *Wozzeck* included. The dance-parody is now not the Waltz but the Tango (bars 39, 181), supported by the incorporation of an alto saxophone in the orchestra; the deployment of tonalistic configurations in both the harmony and the melodic lines of the music is more thorough-going. In fact, the series on which the work is based begins, in the form in which it is first heard, with the complete ascending scale of D minor, in its 'harmonic' form (Example 3a); the remaining notes are ordered so that in the inverted form of the series they arpeggiate the chord of the added sixth, with a jazzy 'blue-note' inflection of the third (Example 3b). Although this series, unlike that of the *Lyric Suite*, does not fall neatly into two halves with clear affiliations to tonal scales a tritone apart, the central sonority of the work is compounded of the major triads of F and B♮ (German H) superimposed, underpinned by a low D♭. The letter names of these triads must be construed as another private reference to Hanna Fuchs, but the sonority itself, and in particular the combination of triads at a distance of exactly half an octave, is fundamental to the tonal characteristics of Berg's late music.

Example 4. *Lulu*: (a) basic series; (b) derivation of Alwa series

Composing *Lulu*

Thus far in his work on *Lulu*, Berg had used a twelve-note series similar to that of the *Lyric Suite* in its neat division into two halves along tonal lines (Example 4a). While sketching and composing music for the opera he had derived scales, chords and motivic patterns from this series – including the near-chromatic fragments associated with the *Hauptrhythmus* (see Example 1b, p. 15) – and this technique for creating material undeniably related to a series yet lying beyond its original confines had also served him well for *Der Wein*. But composing a three-act opera proved inevitably to be a far larger task than writing a concert aria, and by September 1929 Berg was finding his existing pool of musical resources insufficient. In his search for a way of developing his material further he was crucially assisted by Willi Reich, who towards the end of August had drawn Berg's attention to the existence of rows which were identical in their transposed retrograde and inverted forms, and also to 'complementary series' which could be obtained by strict derivation from any given row.[41] The former observation would in due course apply to the series of Berg's next work, the Violin Concerto; the latter was to bring about the immediate enrichment of the musico-dramatic edifice of *Lulu*.

Following systematic procedures of the kind he discussed with Reich, Berg derived a number of 'complementary series' from the original series of the opera, and gave them a musico-dramatic function by associating each of the principal characters of the drama with a specific series. The series of Alwa, for example, was produced by taking every seventh note from cyclically repeating forms of the basic series (Example 4b).[42] But despite this apparently calculating approach, the audible dimension of the music is still rich in thematicism, sonority and late-Romantic gesture. Douglas Jarman has even identified points of reference to tonal centres which suggest a Wagnerian association of keys with characters and ideas.[43] The alliance between the audible and inaudible dimensions of *Lulu* extends deeper than this, however.

Reich had pointed out to Berg that the property whereby the inversion of a series is simultaneously its retrograde is a corollary of a mirror relationship between the pitches (irrespective of their order) which constitute the two halves of the row.[44] He further observed that knowing the first six notes of such a row would allow the order of the remaining six to be deduced, and, more intriguingly, that a partial knowledge of the first hexachord (four or five, say, of the six 'determining tones') would give an ambiguous indication of a number of possible rows. The existence of a group of such rows related through a common area of four or five notes could, he argued, make 'modulation between closely related twelve-note rows possible'. Characteristically, Berg did not lose sight of this idea when he came to employ Reich's other discovery to generate rows for Alwa, Dr Schön and the other characters of the Lulu drama. Such 'common areas' may be seen to link almost all of the opera's many series, constituting a wealth of potential motivic and thematic relationships.[45] From these resources Berg developed a vast range of musico-dramatic meanings, which the ear can readily appreciate whether or not the inaudibly complex procedures underlying their derivation are known.[46]

The proliferation of dramatically functional series was matched by a similarly motivated adoption of traditional formal archetypes. When he resumed work on the opera in the summer of 1930, it was with the exposition of the sonata movement whose sections are distributed across the latter part of Act I and through which Dr Schön's interactions with Lulu unfold. The difficulties of paring down Wedekind's verbose text to make a libretto sufficiently well-ordered for such purposes was one obstacle to speedy progress, and another was the complexity of his new serial method.[47] He was also distracted by the pleasures of driving through the Carinthian countryside in the Ford car which the flow of royalties from Wozzeck had afforded him.[48] It was July 1931 before Act I was finished, and Berg had to resist pressure to finish the work for the 1932–3 season.[49] As he continued with Act II, he built a work of direct and overwhelming dramatic impact, yet whose construction is of a fantastical complexity at all levels, both large and small. As well as Schön's sonata, other sections alluding to formal and generic archetypes participate in a network of variations, developments and recapitulations spread across the opera's vast span. On the broadest scale, the drama of Lulu's rise to power over men and her subsequent persecution is presented as a large-scale palindrome, cutting across the three-act layout but focused on a literally palindromic orchestral interlude, the strictness of whose conception is underlined by its precise correlation with the scenes of a silent film whose scenario is itself symmetrically organised.[50] By mid-November 1931 Berg was past this central turning-point, having composed over 900 bars of Act II,[51] but his work during 1932 was painfully slow and constantly interrupted. Towards the end of the year he and Helene purchased the 'Waldhaus', a new country home, also in Carinthia, in a lakeside setting on the Wörthersee. Conditions were spartan, but the house was habitable in winter, giving Berg the prospect of significantly more time for composition than before. Writing to Schoenberg in December 1932, he told him enthusiastically of his intention to resume his work there early in the following spring.[52]

3

Composition and performance history

By the time Act II of *Lulu* was finished in mid-September 1933, Berg's affairs had suffered a tragic reverse. The accession of the Nazi party to power in Germany led to a ban on performances of works by the Schoenberg school along with those of many other composers, and Schoenberg himself, as a Jew, was forced to flee from Berlin to America. With the performance of much of the music in its catalogue outlawed in Germany and curtailed by sympathetic developments in Austria, the financial position of Universal Edition was undermined by the loss of income from royalties. They could no longer maintain Berg's monthly stipend at its pre-June level of 1,000 schillings and reduced it in stages to half this amount by the end of the year – a loss made all the more severe by rising inflation.[1] But, since Berg had finished nothing since *Der Wein* and was already in debit with UE, even this money represented a generous advance against royalties on music whose prospects of performance were growing ever poorer.

In America, Schoenberg – whose own position was perilous – made efforts to raise money for Berg as well as for himself and his family. Berg hoped that a rich patron of the arts, such as Elizabeth Sprague Coolidge, might be interested in sponsoring *Lulu*, but feared that these plans were unlikely to succeed now that his reputation was no longer maintained by regular performances.[2] In fact, by the spring of 1934 Schoenberg had arranged not only for the Library of Congress to purchase the autograph full score of *Wozzeck*, but also for them to offer Berg a commission for a string quartet.[3] Incredibly, Berg refused this, although the composition of *Lulu* was by now nearly complete after a hard winter's work away from Vienna.[4] He was clearly determined to get the opera ready for performance, and after checking through the completed *Particell* (short score) he proceeded to work on the orchestration from about the beginning of June.[5] A by-product of this stage of his work was the preparation of the five *Symphonische Stücke* (now generally known as the *Lulu Suite*), whose courageous premiere in Berlin under Erich Kleiber at the end of November 1934 precipitated the conductor's resignation

25

from his post and flight from Germany. By the end of March 1935 the suite had also been performed in Prague, Geneva, London and Boston, but this can have done little to relieve Berg's financial position. Worst of all, while the score of *Lulu* was likely to be finished by the end of the year, it was now inconceivable that the opera might be produced in Germany or Austria.[6]

An unexpected commission

Shortly before this, Berg had been approached by a young American violinist with a request for him to compose a concerto. Louis Krasner was in his early thirties, and during a period of study in Vienna had become familiar with the music of the Schoenberg school.[7] He had attended Stokowski's performance of *Wozzeck* in New York and was, on his own admission, 'overwhelmed' by the work.[8] His accompanist in Vienna, Rita Kurzmann, was from 1932 host to Webern's acclaimed series of private lectures, some of which Krasner also attended, and among other things it was her playing of Berg's Piano Sonata which moved him to attempt to overcome the then widespread rejection of the music of Schoenberg, Berg and Webern by audiences and influential performers. When, after a period in America, Krasner returned to Vienna at the beginning of 1935, Frau Dr Kurzmann arranged for him to hear the *Lyric Suite* in a private performance at her home. Krasner, who had already identified Berg in his own mind as the most lyrically inclined of the three composers, now became almost obsessed with the idea of commissioning a concerto from him. He was not to be dissuaded by friends who told him that Berg was unlikely to accept a commission – a reasonable judgement of the composer's mood in view of his rejection of the approach made by the Library of Congress. Berg, for his part, made discreet enquiries about Krasner before agreeing to meet him – Rita Kurzmann no doubt being instrumental in bringing them together – but, once contact was made, the violinist was able to give a tangible indication of his goodwill by arranging for Koussevitsky to schedule a performance of the *Lulu Suite* with his Boston Symphony Orchestra.[9]

Speaking many years later, Krasner himself recalled the meetings which led to Berg's acceptance of the commission:

The personal tone between Berg and myself gradually grew in relaxation and harmony and during a conversation at his home, I soon felt able to broach directly the subject of a full-scale Violin Concerto composed by Alban Berg. The Master's reaction was not unfriendly but he seemed surprised at the idea. The conversation that followed was quite lively: 'You are a young violinist in the beginnings of a promising concert

26

career', he told me. 'What you require for your programs are brilliant compositions by Wieniawski and Vieuxtemps – you know, that is not my kind of music!' My response was not difficult to conceive: 'Meister – Beethoven and Mozart also wrote Violin Concertos.' 'Ah ja', he said softly and smiled. I pursued my momentary vantage and spoke on: 'The attacking criticism of 12-tone music everywhere is that this music is only cerebral and without feeling or emotion. If you undertake to write a Violin Concerto, it certainly will have to be a very serious, deliberate and communicative work for the violin – for the violin is a lyrical and songful instrument which I know you love. Think of what it would mean for the whole Schoenberg Movement if a new Alban Berg Violin Concerto should succeed in demolishing the antagonism of the "cerebral, no emotion" cliché and argument.'[10]

Berg did not respond immediately, but promised to consider Krasner's request in his own time. The violinist meanwhile engaged the support of influential figures including Alfred Kalmus and Hans Heinsheimer of Universal Edition and David Josef Bach of the Vienna Workers' Concert Association. A series of discussions ensued, and eventually Berg, Krasner, Heinsheimer and Bach met in the offices of Universal Edition to finalise the commission.[11] Though Berg agreed – 'both dubiously and happily', as Krasner recalled – to compose the concerto, he warned that it would be 'a long, drawn-out process'.[12] The composer's reluctance is obvious, but it must have been almost impossible for him to refuse a fee of 1,500 dollars[13] in the premises of a publisher with whom he was already seriously in debt.

Although he may thus have accepted the idea of writing a Violin Concerto under a certain amount of pressure, Berg did not simply let it slip from his mind while he attended to *Lulu*. Indeed, with the *concertante* Chorale Variations in Act III scene 1 of the opera still to be orchestrated,[14] immediate work on the Violin Concerto allowed it to become to a very small extent a study for *Lulu*, just as *Der Wein* had been six years earlier.[15] Krasner was now back in America, and it was left to friends to report to him that Berg was attending violin recitals in Vienna; the violinist himself naturally kept in touch with Berg by mail, informing him in particular that he would be spending time in Switzerland during the summer.[16] In response to a telegram from Krasner – perhaps reporting on the Boston performance of the *Lulu Suite* – Berg wrote on 28 March that he would be at the Waldhaus from May and would compose the concerto then; he mentioned in passing how Brahms too had composed his Violin Concerto overlooking the Wörthersee, more than half a century earlier.[17]

It is not clear just how early Berg began to make sketches for the Violin Concerto. In his letter to Krasner, written at the end of March, he claimed

27

to have 'already accomplished a good deal of preparatory work', and Reich's biography of the composer suggests that he 'occupied himself unceasingly with the project' after agreeing to the commission.[18] But Berg's reply to Krasner's telegram has every sign of being a holding letter in response to continuing pressure from a man who had already outmanoeuvred him over the very commissioning of the work. If he did have difficulty in forming a mental image of the piece, this may well have been because of the lack of a poetic motivation behind it.

'To the memory of . . .'

The necessary stimulus came unexpectedly and tragically from the death on 22 April of Manon Gropius, the young and beautiful daughter of Alma Mahler Werfel (the dedicatee of *Wozzeck*) and the great architect Walter Gropius. Alma Schindler (1879–1964) was a gifted and intelligent woman whose remarkable love life led her into romantic associations with several prominent artists of the day: Klimt, Mahler, Kokoschka, Gropius and Franz Werfel. Alma married Gropius on 18 August 1915 and gave birth to Manon on 5 October 1916 after a pregnancy of ten months. Two of her other three children failed to survive infancy and Manon's health was never good; when she contracted polio in April 1934, however, it was both unforeseen and devastating. To her mother, Manon ('Mutzi') was a person of almost other-worldly spiritual beauty: 'She was a fairy-tale being; nobody could see her without loving her . . . She was the most beautiful human being in every sense. She combined all our good qualities. I have never known such a divine capacity for love, such creative power to express and to live it.'[19] At the time she was struck down, the seventeen-year-old Mutzi was beginning to attract the romantic attention of artists, politicians and intellectuals in the Werfels' social circle in much the same way as Alma herself had in her earlier years. Paralysed in the legs, she survived for another year, but died on Easter Monday, 22 April 1935. Her last words to her mother were: 'Let me die . . . You'll get over it, Mummy, as you get over everything – I mean . . . as everyone gets over everything . . .'[20]

After hearing the news, Berg called on Alma to ask her permission to dedicate his new concerto 'To the Memory of an Angel', as a requiem for Mutzi. Soon he was at the Waldhaus composing furiously in the heat of inspiration, his quick progress facilitated by whatever 'preparatory work' he had done earlier in the year. For example, among the sketches preserved in the Österreichische Nationalbibliothek are notations of virtuoso technical

28

Example 5. Violin Concerto series (letter of 28 August 1935, Berg to Schoenberg)

effects – artificial harmonics, double stops and so forth – taken from the concertos of Glazunov and others, scores to which he could hardly have had access in Carinthia.[21] Another sketch – jotted down, like the virtuoso effects, on the full-score paper Berg was using for *Lulu* – indicates that he had probably also decided at an early stage on the division of the concerto into four paired movements ([?2]/4, 3/4; 4/4, 6/8), the last two of which were at first conceived as a Chorale and a Rondo.[22] The very same sheet contains a notation of the concerto's twelve-note series, whose embedded triads, whole-tone scale and chain of fifths – the latter corresponding to the open strings of the violin – Berg later outlined in a letter to Schoenberg (Example 5).[23] And in what was probably the earliest notation for the actual music of the concerto, written on the back of a rather grim twelve-note Prelude for piano by one of his pupils and thus almost certainly done in Vienna, he had developed the bare bones of the series into the first theme (bars 11–20) of Part I (henceforth I/11–20, etc.).[24]

These early sketches should be seen in the context of a larger pattern of work. The composition of the concerto fell into a number of stages, which were by no means absolutely separate from each other but may be delineated schematically for the sake of discussion:

(i)   planning the large- and small-scale form of the work and the character of its sections;

(ii) deriving abstract patterns from the twelve-note series, giving prominence to familiar scales and chords;

(iii) rough-sketching the texture of key passages of the work in line with the decisions about their musical character taken at stage (i);

(iv) sketching the essential thematic material, using both the series and the abstract patterns derived from it at stage (ii);

(v)   composing a continuity draft of the entire work, notating only as much as was necessary to fix the course of the music in conjunction with the sketches of various kinds already made;

(vi) preparing the *Particell* – a generally neat 'short score' of the work, complete in almost every detail but with the orchestral music notated on two or three staves as in a piano reduction;

(vii) preparing the full score of the work by direct transcription of the *Particell*, with the orchestral music now distributed across individual instrumental staves.

Although the general chronological sequence of these stages is apparent, it is clear from other evidence that the design of the second part of the concerto remained undecided even after much of the thematic material had been worked out – and indeed even after the first part had been composed in all essentials. Most of Berg's apparent difficulties concerned the incorporation of musical *objets trouvés* – a Carinthian folk song and a Bach chorale – and in both cases he made efforts to cover his tracks.

As mentioned above, the basic design of the concerto in two parts (I/II) each divided into two movements (a/b) was evidently settled very early on, the distinction between the four movements according to their time-signatures being reminiscent of the rhythmic characterisation of Schigolch (quavers in 4/4), the Acrobat (6/4), the Schoolboy (9/8) and the Marquis (triplet quavers in 3/4) that is found in *Lulu*. On the other hand, both the character and the sequence of the individual movements were originally quite different in conception to the pattern found in the concerto as we know it. Berg's earliest thoughts (see above) formed the basis for a fully developed outline, which was to provide a context for the working-out of some of the thematic material:[25]

Ia	2/4	Introduction, *Andante* free (rhapsodic) – *cresc.* to *ff*
Ib	3/4	cheerful (dreamy) Ländler melody, *Allegretto* ABA (variations on a Carinthian folk song) – ends *pp*
IIa	4/4	Vision (Chorale), *Adagio* ABA (chorale, development, chorale) – *cresc./dim.*
		Cadenza, *Allegro*
IIb	6/8	Rondo finishes *f*

Even at this early stage, therefore, he envisaged the incorporation of both a Carinthian folk song and a chorale of some kind – though Bach's name appears nowhere. Indeed a letter written by Berg's brother Charley to their American friend Frida Semler Seabury after the composer's death suggests that Krasner

Example 6. Early sketch for serial chorale melody
(ÖNB Musiksammlung F 21 Berg 85/II, fol. 35v)

may have asked for a chorale to be incorporated in the work,[26] and a chorale-like melody in minims and semibreves by Berg himself, derived from the work's twelve-note series, is found among the sketches (Example 6).[27] This undoubtedly early sketch is reminiscent of the type of chorale used in the *concertante* Chorale Variations in Act III of *Lulu*, which had of course been composed in short score more than a year previously.

Despite the existence of the serial chorale idea, and although Willi Reich later attested that the Bach chorale-setting Berg eventually used was not decided on until the second week of June 1935,[28] there is ample evidence in the sketches to suggest that the requiem chorale 'Es ist genug' was in the composer's mind far earlier than this. As part of his preliminary work, under the heading 'Akkorde u. Cadenzen' ('Chords and Cadences'), he explored for himself how various patterns of triads and seventh-chords familiar in tonal music could be derived from the concerto's series,[29] while on a similar sheet he studied the extraction of chromatic and whole-tone scale fragments (see Example 9a, p. 38, and Example 18, p. 80).[30] The 'Chords and Cadences' sketch must have been early – it contains the basis of various passages in Part I of the concerto, notably the *ritmico* material from the Allegretto (I/140) – yet within one chord progression Berg may be seen to have inscribed the melody and words of the final phrase of 'Es ist genug'. Another sketch, containing notations similar to those of 'Chords and Cadences', contains music which was eventually to find its way into the first Chorale Variation (II/158–64).[31] One may readily conclude that Berg thought at an early stage of using this chorale melody in some way; it would seem, however, that just how he would use it, and in what musical context, took him far longer to determine.

The revision of the plan of the concerto into its present format, including the adoption of 'Es ist genug', was doubtless guided by programmatic

Example 7. 'Ein Vogel auf'm Zwetschgenbaum

thinking. Berg intended the work as a requiem for Mutzi, and seems to have been concerned to finish it in time for her mother's birthday on 31 August.[32] He oversaw Willi Reich's preparation of a general introduction for publication as a tribute to Alma on that day:

Insofar as a transcription into words is possible at all, the 'tone' – a favourite expression of Berg's – of the whole work may be described as follows: delicate Andante melodies emerge from the rising and falling movement of the introduction. These crystallise into a Grazioso middle section and then dissolve back into the waves of the opening. The Allegretto Scherzo rises from the same background; this part captures the vision of the lovely girl in a graceful dance which alternates between a delicate and dreamy character and the rustic character of a [Carinthian] folk tune. A wild orchestral cry introduces the second main part, which begins as a free and stormy cadenza. The demonic action moves irresistibly towards catastrophe, interrupted once – briefly – by a reserved point of rest. Groans and strident cries for help are heard in the orchestra, choked off by the suffocating rhythmic pressure of destruction. Finally: over a long pedal point – gradual collapse. At the moment of highest suspense and anxiety, the Chorale enters, serious and solemn, in the solo violin. Like an organ the woodwinds answer each verse with the original harmonization of the classical model. Ingenious variations follow, with the original Chorale melody always present as a *cantus firmus*, climbing 'misterioso' from the bass while the solo violin intones a 'plaint' [*Klagegesang*] that gradually struggles towards the light. The dirge grows continually in strength; the soloist, with a visible gesture, takes over the leadership of the whole body of violins and violas; gradually they all join in with his melody and rise to a mighty climax before separating back into their own parts. An indescribably melancholy reprise of the [Carinthian] folk tune 'as if in the distance (but much slower than the first time)' reminds us once more of the lovely image of the girl; then the Chorale, with bitter harmonies, ends this sad farewell while the solo violin arches high over it with entry after entry of the plaint.[33]

This clear and moving programme does not tell the whole story, however. As Douglas Jarman has shown, there are autobiographical references in the work which hint at an additional, secret programme running in parallel with the 'official' Mutzi one.[34]

The clue to this lies in the other musical *objet trouvé* in the concerto, the Carinthian folk song 'Ein Vogel auf'm Zwetschgenbaum' (Example 7), whose words run as follows:

> A bird on the plum tree has wakened me,
>   Tridie, tridie, iri, tulie!
>
> Otherwise I would have overslept in Mizzi's bed,
>   Tridie, ri, tulie!
>
> If everybody wants a rich and handsome girl,
>   Tridie, tridie, iri, tulie!
>
> Where ought the devil take the ugly one?
>   Tridie, ri, tulie!
>
> The girl is Catholic and I am Protestant,
>   Tridie, tridie, iri, tulie!
>
> She will surely put away the rosary in bed!
>   Tridie, ri, tulie![35]

In contrast to the text of 'Es ist genug', which is carefully written out in the score of the concerto at the point where the chorale first appears, the extraordinarily *risqué* text of this song is nowhere hinted at by Berg. But, as Jarman has argued, it is inconceivable that Berg would have quoted the melody of the song without the text also being intended to mean something in its new context. The name 'Mizzi' approximates to Manon Gropius's nickname – somewhat incongruously in this context; but it could also and more accurately have been the familiar name of Marie Scheuchl, who worked as a servant-girl in the Berg household in Carinthia during Alban's youth and whose illegitimate daughter he had fathered in the spring of 1902.[36] Berg was 17 at this time – roughly Mutzi Gropius's age when she developed polio – and it is easy to see how the portrait in music of her carefree youth which forms Part I of the Violin Concerto could do double duty as a self-portrait of the young Alban.

'I have never worked harder in my life'

The transformation of Berg's original outline into a sequence of music in support of both these programmatic ideas involved a number of stages, the order of which may confidently be determined from the evidence of the sketches, together with the testimonies of Krasner and Reich. Part I was composed first, and fairly straightforwardly, in continuity draft, its two sections departing little from the Andante–Allegretto model Berg had earlier devised. Casting the Allegretto in a 6/8 metre meant a change of plan, however, since this movement was originally to have been in 3/4, with 6/8 reserved for a Rondo finale (Part IIb). As the thematic sketches for the Rondo include march-like ('Marcia') material in 3/4 time, together with an angular theme in dotted rhythm, one may infer that Berg simply swapped these ideas around; the decision to use 6/8 for Part Ib is indeed mentioned explicitly in the sketches.[37] But in composing the Allegretto Berg had also abandoned his idea of writing variations on a Carinthian folk song, and it is clear, if nonetheless remarkable, that this at first led him to exclude the folk song altogether. Only when he came to prepare the *Particell* of Part I in detail did he expand the draft, inserting bars I/176-231 – even in the final version a join from I/175 to I/232 is not implausible – and thus restoring both the folk song and its autobiographical connotations.[38] Some details of the concluding Stretta (bars I/240–57) were also left until this stage.

At this point, although Berg had made copious thematic sketches for the Rondo and had provisionally decided to make use of the melody 'Es ist genug', he found it difficult to continue with the concerto. Without divulging his plans any further than was necessary, he enlisted the help of both Krasner and

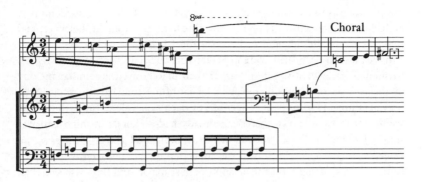

Example 8. Intermediate plan for link from Cadenza to Chorale
(ÖNB Musiksammlung F 21 Berg 85/II fol. 28)

Reich. The violinist was invited to the Waldhaus in early June and played through Part I of the concerto with Berg from the *Particell*, which must therefore have been complete by this time.[39] But the real purpose of the invitation was for Berg to gain inspiration for the Cadenza. Without really telling Krasner why, Berg asked him to 'play' – not concertos, not sonatas, just play – while he busied himself elsewhere. Krasner was delighted:

Since my student days I [had] always loved to spend my evenings . . . playing and improvising for myself . . . Now, at this high moment, the great composer was asking me to relive the hidden long hours of my youthful years. I played and played – for hours it seemed – whatever strange figurations, chords, passages [passagework], pizzicati and impulsive combinations on the violin – everything that chance brought to my fingers, bow and mind. After an hour or more when, without stopping, I lapsed into a section of a Concerto, Berg interrupted me and called from the other room, 'Nein, bitte, keine Konzerte, nur spielen – präludieren sie nur weiter – unbedingt!' No, please, no Concertos – just continue to play![40]

From this and perhaps other material, Berg was able to draft the music which eventually became bars II/7–18. In defiance of his original plan for Part II, however, he then sketched a link directly from this point to the chorale melody, which was to open in C major through a resolution of the dominant seventh chord on G outlined at the end of the Cadenza (Example 8). But he seems almost immediately to have had second thoughts about this tonality, opting instead for D major – a traditional key for violin concertos, used by Mozart (K. 211, K. 218), Beethoven, Brahms and Tchaikovsky – and thinking that the sustained A in the orchestra at bar II/17 should now serve as the bass of the functional dominant chord. Correspondingly, the scalar 'pre-echo' of the chorale was to be transposed a tone higher to G–A–B–C♯. The violin part he had already sketched fits poorly into this harmonic context, however, and Berg seems for the moment to have set the whole idea aside.

In the meanwhile, he had evidently taken the crucial decision to quote Bach's harmonisation of 'Es ist genug' rather than merely use the familiar melody of the chorale in some other way. The faithful Reich had therefore been prevailed upon to search out collections of Bach's chorale settings, though he seems not to have known that Berg already had a chorale in mind and was simply looking for Bach's version of it.[41] In both the Cantata *O Ewigkeit, du Donnerwort* (BWV 60, 1723) and the collection of chorales from which Berg copied Bach's setting,[42] the music appears in A major, and Berg also sketched his own serial harmonisation of the melody at this pitch level.[43] The transposition of the chorale to B♭ major came in the wake of a major structural revision to Part II: having at first proposed the pattern Chorale–Cadenza–Rondo, and then devised music to link the Cadenza to the Chorale, Berg finally decided to interpolate some of the Rondo material between the Cadenza and Chorale sections (beginning at bar II/23).[44] He thus abandoned the Mahlerian idea of a Rondo-finale in favour of a sequence whose programmatic basis was explicit, as the 'Marcia' music took on connotations of 'groaning' [*Stöhnen*] in the sketches.[45]

Working quickly – his compositional process seems at this stage to have come perilously close to one of improvisation as he assembled the continuity draft piecemeal on the back of sheets which were no longer needed – Berg developed the pounding 'Marcia' music back towards the dominant pedal, which he intended at one stage to be on a low D before deciding on F for the pedal and B♭ major for the chorale.[46] The rhythm of the 'Marcia' now emerged as the *Hauptrhythmus* of the concerto: both its reappearance above the pedal point (II/104–19) and the giant climactic chord (II/125) could be sketched in general terms. Through this realignment of material, Berg had set a context for the introductory words of the chorale – 'It is enough! Lord, when it pleases Thee, relieve me of my yoke!' He made a note to himself that the general design of the transition to the chorale melody, first sketched in C major, should be retained in its new setting.

Berg's early thoughts on the internal organisation of the Chorale section (then intended as Part IIa) had included a plan for it to be in ternary form, with the second A section presenting the music of the first in retrograde, as in the *Allegro misterioso* of the *Lyric Suite*. In this scheme, the first A section was to feature three soloists: double bass, cello and solo violin, supported by chorale harmonies; then the soloist, playing *pianissimo*, was to be joined by the leader (concertmaster) of the orchestra, and as the music proceeded into the B section they were to be joined by half the first violins, then by the other half, and then by the second violins, in a development of the chorale melody, supported by a pizzicato accompaniment (presumably from the violas, cellos and double basses).[47] Although the near-palindromic ABA outline of this section was abandoned as the work took shape, the inspired conception whereby from bar II/170 the soloist gradually takes over the leadership of the upper strings of the orchestra evidently originated at this early stage. This is a moving gesture, unmatched in the concerto literature, yet its significance remains imprecise in the context of the completed work, perhaps because it was conceived before the programme was devised. In other respects, however, the programmatic basis of Part II is clear, and the reprise of the Carinthian folk song confirms that the sequence of catastrophe and transfiguration had an element of autobiography to it. This does not necessarily imply that Berg had a premonition of his death: the character of the work meant that it was likely to be used as his own requiem whether he wished it or not, and it would have been entirely in character for him to have composed the details of the music in such a way as to make this use legitimate.

Apart from matters of design, the sketches confirm that Berg's compositional method gave primacy to thematic resources, rather than to the series as such. Typical was his procedure in composing the 'Trio II' section of Part I (beginning at bar I/155). Having earlier isolated a rising chromatic scale by partitioning a cyclically permutated version of the series into groups of 3, 5 and 4 notes (Example 9a),[48] he reverted to the original starting-point of the inverted series to produce, by a similar partition into groups of 3 notes, 4 notes and 5, the characteristic motive of the Trio material with its supporting harmonies (Example 9b).[49] The second bar of the phrase was derived by applying the same partition to the prime form of the series (Example 9c), so that the two complementary bars were related by inversion – a highly characteristic procedure of Berg's phrase construction.

This material was now sufficient for his immediate purpose: in composing the continuity draft he would be able to refer to it on its various appearances and reappearances by its melodic line only; it could always be copied into the *Particell*, perhaps from memory (and transposed as appropriate) from the preliminary sketch. Thus, in the continuity draft, bars I/155 and I/156 are virtually empty: the detailed composition continues at the point where the material is developed – initially with reference to the series, as a kind of continuation, then freely dwelling on a falling chromatic scale fragment. This process is exactly in line with the principle of 'liquidation' outlined by

Example 9. Composition sketches for Trio II theme

Schoenberg in the context of classicist musical phraseology:

> [After] a phrase and its repetition [the] technique to be applied in the continuation is a kind of development, comparable in some respects to the condensing technique of 'liquidation'. Development implies not only growth, augmentation, extension and expansion, but also reduction, condensation and intensification . . .
>
> Liquidation consists in gradually eliminating characteristic features, until only uncharacteristic [i.e. un-characterised] ones remain, which no longer demand a

Example 10. I/154–5: Interaction of serial forms in final version

continuation.

    . . . The end of liquidation is generally marked by a combination of repose and suspense . . . in anticipation of the re-entrance of the theme. At this point, the retarding effect of a pedal point is appropriate . . . it can also be a sustained or repeated note in another voice.[50]

After a six-bar phrase which dissolves into superimpositions of the 'uncharacterised' chromatic descent, bars I/161–2 and the reprise of the theme at bar I/163 illustrate Schoenberg's procedure exactly.

As Example 10 illustrates, the final version in the *Particell* in fact shows some adjustment to the sketched material in bar I/155 in order to effect a join from the end of the previous section. Indeed, small adjustments to the strictly serial derivation of the music occur throughout the concerto. Frequently these would seem to be in order to avoid the bare sonority of octaves between contrapuntal parts, but there are other deviations from serial exactitude which are not motivated by this purpose. There is in fact a good deal of internal evidence to suggest that Berg was careless in copying from the *Particell* into the full score, and even from the sketches and continuity draft into the *Particell*. The most serious result of this was the publication of a hopelessly incorrect version of the solo part in II/4–5 from Berg's full score (the correct text, taken from the *Particell*, is shown in Example 11); there are numerous smaller examples.[51] Such lapses must be distinguished, however, from

Example 11. Authentic text of bars II/4–5 (from Berg's *Particell*)

instances where thematic material is repeated or developed without reference
to its serial origins, as in the four-part canon for solo violin at the centre of
Part IIa (II/78–90), or, more subtly, in the reprise of the 'Marcia' (II/111–19).
While there is little doubt that the score of the concerto as originally published
contains numerous points of error and uncertainty, the resolution of these is
not an easy matter for musicologists or performers.[52] The work is less strictly
serial than *Lulu*, and many notes which appear questionable in the light of
serial analysis are actually confirmed by the continuity draft – a manuscript
source which necessarily has little likelihood of including errors arising from
the transcription of material between one stage of the compositional process
and the next.

Having finished the concerto in *Particell* on 15 July,[53] Berg proceeded with
the orchestral score. But since Krasner had already seen Part I during his visit
in June, it seemed best to begin with Part II, so that this could be sent to the
violinist in *Particell* as soon as possible.[54] In this final stage of his work on the
concerto, Berg was dealing with a notably smaller orchestra than in *Lulu*,
lacking the colouristic potential of the opera's piano and vibraphone, but
retaining the characteristic alto saxophone, which he had first introduced in
Der Wein. In fact, the orchestra of the Violin Concerto is virtually identical
to that of the aria. The textures of the concerto are less precisely drawn,
however, than those of its predecessors: the climax of section IIa, around bar
II/125, is not projected with the lurid colours of Lulu's death, nor does section
Ib dance as lightly as the central section of *Der Wein* – or as heavily as the
aria's Tango pastiche. In the end, the marvellously volatile scoring of the

concertante Chorale Variations in *Lulu* owed no specific textures to the concerto's example. In general, the Violin Concerto's function as a requiem is matched by its restrained colours, with the saxophone and brass kept on a tight rein. The quotation of Bach's chorale-setting, scored for three clarinets and bass clarinet in imitation of a small church organ, epitomises this restraint, by comparison with the sleazy mouth-organ, circus-organ and barrel-organ which Berg chose to imitate in *Lulu*.

It seems likely that the orchestration of Part II was completed earlier than expected. Berg wrote again to Krasner on 27 July, asking after his plans and once more expressing his hope that the violinist would visit him to settle the violin part, and one may infer that this letter accompanied the promised *Particell* of Part II, since the entire score was finished by the second week in August. From the available evidence, it would seem that the orchestration was completed on the 12th, the *Particell* of Part I was sent to Krasner on the 13th and the full score of the entire work to Universal Edition on 14th.[55] Krasner eventually saw Berg again on 16 September, a visit which probably prompted a last-minute revision to bars I/77–8.[56] Thus the general chronology of the composition becomes clear: one may reasonably assume that after his preliminary work on the overall design of the work and the abstract properties of the series Berg spent much of May on the continuity draft of Part I; that in the light of his difficulties over the design of Part II he proceeded to assemble the *Particell* of Part I until early in June; that Part II was nevertheless sorted out in continuity draft within a month of this and put into *Particell* by 15 July. This would suggest that Helene Berg's assertion that the work was composed in six weeks was not altogether an exaggeration,[57] and that Berg's touching remark to Krasner – 'I have never worked harder in my life, and, what's more, the work gave me increasing pleasure' – was entirely justified.[58]

A posthumous premiere

Berg's health had been poor for many years: he had a tendency to develop abscesses and suffered badly from asthma and hay-fever. As he worked on the concerto his asthma returned, accompanied by heart trouble;[59] he also developed toothache.[60] Yet he felt compelled to press on with his new work, as Krasner's testimony vividly relates:

Frau Helene Berg recounted to me again and again how Alban, ill in bed and tortured with pain, worked frantically and without interruption to conclude the composition of his Violin Concerto. Refusing to stop for food or sleep, he drove his hand relentlessly and in fever. 'I must continue', Berg responded to his wife's pleadings, 'I cannot stop – I do not have time.'[61]

Worse was to come, when, as he put the finishing touches to the concerto and returned to the orchestration of *Lulu*, a wasp-sting he suffered at the base of the spine developed – over 'a crescendo lasting several days' – into a fearful abscess.[62] By the 26th, as he explained in a letter to Reich, he had been forced to seek medical treatment:

So right now I am in Velden, where the doctor has again tortured me frightfully. On account of the insect poison, the matter has evidently grown to far greater proportions than is normal with a carbuncle. There is almost constant pain: I suppose that is only to be expected![63]

It was perhaps on Dr Engstler's advice that he decided not to travel to Prague for the ISCM Festival, which began without him on 1 September.[64] The doctor's treatment was effective, in that the abscess now healed completely; but Berg soon developed a number of tiny pustules which made sitting painful.[65] These too disappeared after treatment – Krasner appears to have found nothing remiss when he visited the composer on 16 September – yet the condition itself was by no means cured. In October Berg developed severe blisters after a walk, one of which became so painfully infected that walking was difficult.[66] But despite the constant strain on his morale, he was still thinking of new composition plans, as he told Helene.[67] He had earlier discussed with Willi Reich his ideas for a third string quartet, a piece of chamber music with piano, a symphony (!), and possibly works for radio and film.[68]

By early November, however, his spirits were at a low ebb. When a new carbuncle appeared above his coccyx, Berg – no longer able to afford his usual doctor's fee – went to another, who gave him morphine.[69] From a letter written to Reich on the 4th it is clear that his health, though poor, was now only one of a number of difficulties he faced:

. . . somehow we *must* get help! . . . I have enough to live on for one, maybe two months, but what then? My mind is on nothing else and, thinking it over, I am deeply depressed. Healthwise I am also at something of a low ebb, but that problem is moderate by comparison.[70]

In addition to the morphine, Berg was also finding relief from the painful symptoms of his condition by secretly taking large doses of aspirin.[71] Soon after he returned to Vienna on 12 November he was facing the prospect of selling the Waldhaus, something he dreaded, since, as he explained to Schoenberg, he had done more work there in the past two years than he had achieved elsewhere in the previous ten; moreover, his physical and financial distress was compounded by the disillusionment he felt at being no longer considered 'a native in his fatherland'.[72] As he wrote these words, at the end of November, Berg was again 'in a recumbent position' on account of the carbuncle; he was able, nevertheless, to attend the final rehearsals and Vienna premiere of the *Lulu Suite*, which took place on 11 December. Helene Berg's response to her husband's condition was to lance him with a pair of scissors sterilised in boiling water – an action which may well have hastened the onset of blood poisoning.[73] On Saturday 14th, despite his feverish condition, Berg went through the piano score of the Violin Concerto with Rita Kurzmann, who had appropriately been entrusted with the task of preparing the reduction.[74] Two days later the pain suddenly eased, but by the evening he was running a temperature of over 40 degrees; a doctor was called, but as the carbuncle on Berg's back seemed to be fading, and no further abscesses were visible, he attributed the composer's temperature to influenza.[75] Berg was admitted to the Rudolfspital the next day, but two exploratory operations, one immediate and another the following day, failed to locate a central source of infection; transfusions were needed to restore the loss of blood.[76] Drugs kept Berg's strength up for a few days, but on the Sunday his heart weakened; the next day bore his fateful number, 23, and he regained consciousness that morning, saying calmly that the day would indeed be decisive.[77] At the end, as he struggled for breath, he recalled the words of the chorale: 'Es ist genug, es ist genug!'; then, calmly: 'Now we will all sleep – you, Helene – my sister and I – we will all sleep.'[78] He died of general septicaemia in the small hours of Tuesday 24 December 1935 and was buried four days later in his home suburb of Hietzing.[79] The post-mortem revealed a distended spleen and abscesses in the lungs, kidneys and prostate.[80]

It had been intended that the Violin Concerto should receive its premiere at the 1937 Festival of the ISCM, but Webern now travelled to Barcelona in his capacity as president of the Society's Vienna group, in the hope of persuading the Festival committee to schedule the work for the 1936 Festival, which was to take place in that city in April. He returned to Vienna on 4 January with this precious task accomplished.[81] The ISCM contacted Krasner in America and he arranged for Rita Kurzmann to travel there so that they could work together in the brief period of time available. The evening before they sailed for Europe, they played through the concerto privately in New

York for Leopold Godowsky and Mischa Elman.[82] In Vienna, Krasner and Kurzmann worked with Webern, who was to conduct the first performance, and they gave another private preview of the work on 8 April.[83]

Webern now began to have doubts about his ability to go through with the task, and only an ultimatum from Krasner persuaded him to travel to Barcelona.[84] The two men arranged their train journey to take them through Germany, so as to gain a first-hand impression of the country under Nazi rule. Webern's emotional involvement with Berg's last score undermined the rehearsals from the start: in contrast to the successful relationship he had enjoyed with the Pau Casals Orchestra four years earlier, he found it impossible to communicate his precise wishes to the musicians, and became nervous and angry. After the third and final rehearsal he locked himself in his hotel room, saying that the performance could not take place. Now it was Helene Berg's turn to plead with him: only when she knelt weeping before him did he surrender the score. With the premiere due to take place the following day, a lucky chance found Hermann Scherchen, who had premiered the *Three Fragments from Wozzeck* and *Der Wein*, also engaged at the Festival; Scherchen went through the work in his hotel room with Krasner and borrowed half an hour of orchestral rehearsal, during which he demanded that Krasner play his part from memory, telling him that 'One does not play a thing like this from the music.' Scherchen's inspirational conducting saved the performance, which took place as scheduled on 19 April 1936.[85] The young Benjamin Britten, who was present, described the work immediately as 'great – Best of the festival'.[86]

Later performances

One of the conditions of Krasner's commission was that he would initially retain the performing rights to the concerto, and all the early performances therefore featured him as soloist. At the concerto's second performance, on 1 May 1936 in London, Webern redeemed himself by his musicianship: according to Krasner, 'Webern was the inspirational Master on the conductor's podium, the orchestra was at one with him and the performance became a Devotion for all.'[87] The Vienna premiere on 25 October 1936, under Otto Klemperer, was overshadowed by the worsening political situation, which branded as unacceptable not only Berg's music but also Krasner and Klemperer, who were Jews. Both official pressure and opposition among the orchestral players threatened the performance, but Klemperer held out, saying that if the work were dropped he would refuse to conduct the concert at all and might even choose to leave Vienna for good. The conductor's magnetic personality and box-office drawing power won the day, and the antagonistic voices within the orchestra were countered by the singular decision of the senior concertmaster, Arnold Rosé, to participate in the orchestral accompaniment to a violin concerto. But, in Krasner's words:

. . . the direct counterstroke of the Philharmonic musicians – unprecedented, unimaginable, and of historic dimensions – was yet to come. As the Concerto's concluding high tones for solo violin and fading soft chords for orchestra melted away to an eerie silence – and almost before any applause could be heard – the entire orchestra membership arose as if on command, turned abruptly, and marched suddenly off the stage. Otto Klemperer and I were left aghast and alone to turn and acknowledge the response of the audience. We were alone, but for one notable and extremely significant exception. Arnold Rosé stood up and remained erect, standing tall and solitary by his Concertmaster's chair. He applauded and gripped our hands . . .[88]

Other early performances in Europe were in Paris (under Charles Munch), in Brussels (under Jascha Horenstein), and then a highly successful repeat performance in London on 9 December, this time under Sir Henry Wood's baton, at which Walter Gropius was present. After the performance, when Krasner was alone in his dressing room:

. . . a tall, silent gentleman, with clear, fixed eyes came through the open door and walked across the room to me. He nodded his head, shook my hand and said, 'I am Walter Gropius. Thank you'. My breath stopped short, I was so shaken. We faced each other for a full minute, or perhaps two – not a word was spoken. In Walter Gropius I saw before me his daughter, Manon, his friend Alban, Vienna and its decade of years gone by. Finally, before I could recover my composure, Gropius turned and measuredly . . . retraced his steps out of the room . . .[89]

After this, performances followed at the Maggio Musicale in Florence under Mario Rossi and in Stockholm under Fritz Busch. The latter, like the first London performance, was recorded, but neither was issued commercially at the time. In the United States, Krasner performed the concerto with Koussevitsky in Boston and New York, with Stokowski in Philadelphia, with Frederick Stock in Chicago, Artur Rodzinski in Cleveland and with Dimitri Mitropoulos in Minneapolis. With Rodzinski he also made the first commercial recording of the work, for Columbia Records, in 1940.[90]

After the war, the concerto was taken up by other violinists, including Joseph Szigeti, who recorded it with Mitropoulos in 1945.[91] The first German performance was given in Frankfurt by Gustav Lenszewski, conducted by Bruno Vondenhoff, on 24 November 1946,[92] and the concerto was performed as part of a fortnight of Austrian music in Paris in 1948, along with the *Three Fragments from Wozzeck*, the Chamber Concerto and the *Lyric Suite*.[93] Further recordings came in 1954 from both André Gertler (with Paul Kletzki) and Ivry Gitlis (with William Strickland).[94] The growth of the concerto's reputation during the 1950s is illustrated by its billing in two London Proms. In 1955 it was thought necessary to include Beethoven's Seventh Symphony in the same concert as the Berg, to ensure good attendance, but four years later the concerto was given under the title 'Masters of the Twentieth Century'.[95] Henryk Szeryng took the work to Warsaw in 1958, and Isaac Stern recorded it with Bernstein in 1962. During the 1960s the concerto established its place in the repertoire of the world's leading soloists, and its later discography was to include notable performances by Josef Suk, Yehudi Menuhin (with Boulez), Arthur Grumiaux, Kyung Wha Chung (with Solti), Pinchas Zukerman (again with Boulez), Itzhak Perlman (with Ozawa) and Gidon Kremer. Inevitably, but unfortunately, none of these fine players was in a position to correct the garbled text of the solo part in II/4–5, which affects the character of the opening of this movement profoundly. Their recordings also illustrated that the text of the unaccompanied cadenza (II/78–90) was problematic in its attempt to make the underlying four-part canon practicable in performance.[96] The performance history of the concerto awaited the new lease of life which would come when a critical edition of the performing materials allowed virtuosi and conductors to work with a score that more precisely reflected Berg's intentions.

4

Form, materials and programme

As is the case in the other works of Berg's maturity, the layout of the Violin Concerto is best understood against a background of formal conventions familiar from the music of the Classic and Romantic eras. This does not imply that the music merely conforms to the outlines of, say, textbook sonata or rondo forms; on the contrary, key features of such stereotypes are placed in focus just sufficiently for the listener to be alert to the ongoing play of near-repetitions, developments, variations and near-recapitulations by which the music renews and constantly expands its range of cross-reference. In this respect, the concerto exhibits a greater degree of freedom of association than the works between *Wozzeck* and *Lulu*, and reflects the gains in compositional technique which underpin the latter opera's sophisticated interaction between the libretto's dramatic and textual structure and the musical forms deployed in setting it.

In a letter to Schoenberg, dated 28 August 1935, Berg himself described the division of the concerto into two parts, each with two movements:[1]

> I   a) Andante (Prelude)
>   b) Allegretto (Scherzo)
>
> II a) Allegro (Cadenza)
>   b) Adagio (Chorale Variations)

This doubly bipartite design was unusual for Berg, who had previously shown a marked preference for ternary structures – as the three acts of *Lulu*, the three sections of *Der Wein*, the three movements of the Chamber Concerto, the three acts of *Wozzeck* and the set of Three Orchestral Pieces all testify. Thus eschewing the ready emergence of an arch-like aspect from a ternary design,[2] he also dispensed with literal palindromes for the first time in a major work since *Wozzeck*. But, just as the formal devices employed in the earlier works had been programmatically motivated, so the concerto's superficially unexpected design was a response to a programme which, like that of the *Lyric Suite*, excluded large-scale circularity. The sequence of gaiety, tragedy and transfiguration is essentially irreversible, and its musical analogue was structured accordingly. At the same time, both the quartet and the concerto depict a sense of loss through nostalgic musical reminiscence, and the 'loss' in each case ultimately implies some sort of return to an initial *tabula rasa*.

If, as one might expect, such programmatic considerations also dictated the individual formal models for each of the four movements, in no case are the associations which arise so unexpectedly profound as those which come in *Lulu* from the conjunction of sonata form with the confrontational Schön and rondo form with the ineffectually obsessive Alwa. On the contrary, whether through haste or deliberation, the logic of Berg's decisions in the concerto is surprisingly transparent – and perhaps increasingly so as the work progresses. While the prefatory function of the opening Andante is fulfilled as much by the generic expectation of a sonata design at the beginning of the work as by any adherence of the music itself to that archetype, the carefully emphasised sense of recapitulation at bar I/84 signals closure very much in the manner of a symphonic opening movement.[3] The portrayal of carefree youth in movement Ib – whether in relation to Manon or to Berg and his servant-girl – is also straightforwardly achieved, through both the dance-like quality of the music and the quotation of an amorous folk song. And in Part II, the depth of feeling expressed in the music owes far less to the blatant model of resolution (from the shifting sands of a composed-out cadenza to the security of a set of chorale variations) than to the transcendental fusion of form and fantasy in the former and the stylistic ambivalence of the latter.

In this context, it is evident that such cross-references as do occur between the movements are programmatically more significant than the form-building patterns of variation and reprise to be found within them. Easily the most conspicuous of these cross-references are the reprise of the Carinthian folk tune towards the end of movement IIb (II/200) and the reappearance of music from the second Trio of movement Ib at the eye of the storm (II/44) in the Allegro – a movement which also makes numerous briefer references to the others. None of the bolder cross-references in the work represents simply a circularity of form which might be said to satisfy latent musical criteria, as do the return of the introductory material at the end of Ia and the brief returns to the opening material of the Scherzo before both Trio I and the Waltz. But even such internal reprises, which articulate the sense of form within the movements, are more acutely focused in their re-presentation of previously heard material than are the developing variations which Berg habitually substitutes for strict repetitions as phrases are combined into formal units.[4]

At a smaller level still, however, the phrases themselves are frequently built through the sequential repetition of two-bar, one-bar or half-bar units; repetitions based on the inversion of such units also find their place at this level.[5] Thus these two kinds of process – repetition and development – characterise two levels of the moment-by-moment musical organisation – phrase-building and form-building. The result is that those moments which stand outside this hierarchy acquire significance, and while repetition at the form-building level can signify a purely musical conceit – the classical reprise – any subsequent cross-reference, inevitably lying beyond the boundary established through that articulation of formal closure, acquires a more problematic significance which the mind will tend to resolve programmatically. At a larger level still, it is the correlation between the essentially developmental dynamic of the concerto and the unidirectional aspect of the published programme which makes that programme a viable context within which such resolutions may be achieved.

Synopsis

A tabular overview of the formal layout of each movement of the work, as is given below, both elucidates and obscures: elucidates, because it allows patterns of development and recall to be seen synoptically; obscures, because this synoptic view fails to represent the fluidity of the musical memory as it responds to successive nuances of development and recall in real-time listening. Each overview is therefore followed by a brief commentary, chronologically organised and expanding on the schematic identification of thematic and motivic materials – [1], [2], [3i], etc., the 'i' suffix indicating inversion – in the tabular synopses.

Movement Ia (Andante)

I/...	material	length		
1–10	[1]	10 bars	Introduction	10 bars
11–20	[2, 3]	10 bars	A (aaba)	27 bars
21–27	[2, 3i]	7 bars		
28–31	[4, 4]	4 bars		
32–37	[2, 3, 3i]	6 bars		
38–46	[5, 5i]	9 bars	B (abab)	39 bars
47–53	[6, 7]	7 bars		
54–62	[5, 5i]	9 bars		
63–76	[6, 7]	14 bars		

77–80	[4i, 4i]	4 bars	retransition	7 bars
81–83	[3]	3 bars		
84–91	[2, 2, 2]	8 bars	A'	20 bars
92–93	[1]	2 bars		
94–103	[1]	10 bars	(codetta/transition)	

I/1–10 (Introduction) This passage establishes the Andante tempo and the duple metre, together with a characteristic sonority of clarinets, plucked strings (harp) and solo violin which is to reappear at intervals throughout the work. The musical material [1] is a motivic arpeggio pattern alluding to the open strings of the violin.[6] Its development is pursued separately by the clarinets and the soloist, and the constant alternation between them serves to destabilise the tonal sense of both strands – an effect of chiaroscuro that is signalled at the outset by the clarinets' transposition on B♭ being given priority over the violin's more evocative G–D–A–E.

I/11–37 (A) The cadence at I/10–11 is the first of many in the work in which the clear articulation achieved through a nuance of tempo and a change of texture is counterbalanced by a continuity of musical material across the barline;[7] here it is the change of harmony that is minimal (C^9–Gm). Themes [2] and [3] are introduced as antecedent (I/11, double bass) and consequent (I/15, solo violin); [2] is clear in harmonic outline but elusive in melodic content, whereas [3] has a clear melodic contour but is supported by a muddy wholetone chord – at a point where the series would also have permitted a plain dominant 9th chord on C♯.

The second strophe (I/21) is approached via a cadence whose tonal clarity (G^7–Cmaj^7) must be balanced against its evidently localised formal significance. This strophe uses a variant of [2] based on the inverted series, and the subsequent presentation of [3] in literal inversion exposes an upward leap in its concluding gesture (I/27), creating a three-note motive [4]. The clearly directed harmonic motion of I/24–7 is evaded at the cadence by a resolution onto a $D^{Ø7}$ chord (I/28), above which the flute juxtaposes descending and ascending forms of [4], and, as the violin's pursuit of the idea (I/30) is counterpointed by [3i] in the cellos, the accompanying clarinets introduce the first hint of a triplet rhythm.

The reprise of [2] at I/32 is hardly perceptible as such, not only because it moves at twice the original speed, but because the variant from I/21 (double bass, horns) is counterpointed at a crotchet's distance by the original [2] (solo violin, clarinets); each version is played a semitone lower than before. As the soloist regains the upper register (I/34), the contrabassoon and bassoons play theme [3]; the soloist's counterpoint [3i] begins a bar later, but in triplet quavers, so that the theme occupies three bars instead of four. As these rising and falling lines converge towards the middle register, the harmonic support in the centre of the texture evaporates, leaving a bare two-part counterpoint at I/37.

I/38–76 (B) The application of the triplet rhythm to theme [3] has given a new character to the motive [4], which now comprises four notes, and it is this idea which forms the basis of the next phrase [5]. The inversion of melodic contour as [5] gives way to [5i] in the middle of I/42 is matched by a rhythmic 'inversion', whereby the three triplet quavers no longer occupy a position of metrical stress but instead form an anacrusis to the long notes. The orchestral accompaniment meanwhile regains a regular harmonic rhythm which articulates bar I/47 as a point of arrival. Here the motion again quickens, from triplets to semiquavers: the soloist's angular theme [6] is imitated at a crotchet's distance by the flute and enlarged on (from I/51) by the orchestral first violins and violas [7].

The violas hand over in turn to the cellos (I/54), which in a second appearance of [5] and [5i] take the role played by the soloist at I/38, while the violin's accompanying imitation follows the pattern of the flute part at I/47. As the soloist's pace quickens yet again, from semiquavers to sextuplets (I/63), the orchestral music on the contrary slows down, presenting [6] and [7] at half their previous speed. The sequence of horn, trumpet and trombone translates to the brass the previous string orchestration of this melodic line.

I/77–83 (retransition) The quaver motion established by the half-speed repetition of [6] and [7] allows the music to dovetail into [4i] at I/77, with a characteristic use of the inverted material to avoid literal repetition. In line with the undermining of cadential articulations identified earlier in the movement is the *Eroica*-like appearance of theme [3] (I/81, solo violin) in advance of the recapitulation of the A section in which it was first heard. Here, the theme is decorated by lazy appoggiaturas, which by I/83 have liquidated its rhythm entirely, leading into the regular pulse of the reprise.

I/84–103 (A') Just as the thematic sequence of the retransition has brought back [4] and [3] in retrograde order, so the reprise continues this pattern with theme [2]. This is played successively faster, transposed upwards by a fifth each time, and the pulse quickens from minims through crotchets to quavers, which thus merge with the motion of the accompaniment: at I/92, the unified quaver motion, the progression through successive fifths and the thematic sequence are fulfilled in a return to the material of the introduction [1]. In the codetta, varied repetitions of this material eventually settle on a low D as a point of tonal orientation; together with the rhythmic foreshortening which introduces a triple metre at I/102, this produces another cadence by anticipation, leading to the 6/8 Allegretto through a constant quaver pulse.

Movement Ib (Allegretto)

I/...	material	length		
104–109	[8, 8, 9, 9]	6 bars	Scherzo (abcba)	33 bars
110–117	[10, 10, 11, 12, 13]	8 bars		
118–125	[14, 14i]	8 bars		
126–131	[10, 10, 13]	6 bars		
132–136	[8]	5 bars	(codetta)	
137–141	[15, 16, 17]	4½ bars	Trio I (aba)	18 bars
141–150	[15, 16, 17]	9½ bars		
151–154	[15]	4 bars		
155–160	[18]	6 bars	Trio II (aba)	12 bars
161–162	[19]	2 bars		
163–166	[18]	4 bars		
167–172	[15, 16]	6 bars	Trio I	9 bars
173–175	[8]	3 bars	(codetta)	
176–187	[20, 21, 21, 21]	12 bars	Waltz	38 bars
188–199	[11, 12, 13]	12 bars		
200–207	[14, 14i]	8 bars		
208–213	[8, 22, 22]	6 bars	(transition)	
214–227	[23, 23]	14 bars	Folk song	14 bars
228–239	[19i, 19, 24]	12 bars	Coda	30 bars
240–245	[17, 17, 17]	6 bars		
246–257	[19, 24]	12 bars		

I/104–136 (Scherzo) The violinist's musings on G, F# and F♮ (I/94–103) are also continued across the cadence into the upper line of the first Allegretto theme [8] (I/104, clarinets), while the pizzicato accompaniment and the immediate imitation of the theme by the soloist (I/106) recall the sequence of sonorities at the opening of the work. The range of sonority expands to arco strings and a pair of oboes in the continuation [9] (I/108), which the violin again imitates (I/109), whereupon the range of material is developed through a markedly 'Viennese' motive [10] (I/110, violins, I/111, soloist) and its continuation [11] (I/112), standing in urban contrast to the *rustico* theme [12], [13] which follows (I/114, I/116).

At bar I/118 the by now pervasive semiquaver motion gives way to the quaver pulse of a *tranquillo* episode; the B^9 harmony here is static rather than merely stable, supporting the violin's theme [14] yet failing to confirm the sense of directed motion arising from its familiar melodic contour and dance-like rhythm. The theme is answered by its own inversion, the turning-point at I/122 marking an apex within the Scherzo as the thematic elements return in something like reverse order. This sequence ends in the codetta with a reminiscence of [8] (I/132, horns, solo violin), which is extended through a counterpoint of tritone-related triadic arpeggios between the soloist and the cellos.

I/137–154 (Trio I) Three motives [15], [16], [17] are introduced (I/137, I/139, I/140), the last of these being a characteristic *ritmico* figure for the brass. The second phrase (I/141), though similarly constructed to the first through the succession of these materials, is much extended and builds to a forceful tutti (I/147), so lending the abbreviated third phrase (I/151) the illusory character of a reprise. The cadence into Trio II is again carefully articulated both through nuances of tempo – there is a written-out rallentando in the final statement of [15] (I/153) – and by a clear change of texture across the bar-line, but this effect is simultaneously undermined through the soloist's anticipation of theme [18] (I/154).

I/155–166 (Trio II) After the thematic characteristics of [18] have been liquidated through bars I/158–60 (see pp. 37–9), the two-bar Liberamente [19] follows the pattern of the earlier *tranquillo* in combining static harmony with energetic solo figuration (I/161–2). Formally, this is the apex of the entire Scherzo-and-Trio movement – again, cf. the *tranquillo* – but there is no suggestion of a literal palindrome, even at this mid-point, and the Schoenbergian principle of developing variation is maintained as the soloist's arabesques continue through a varied reprise of [18] (I/163).

I/167–175 (Trio I) An abbreviated reprise of the first Trio is led by the tuba (later trombone), with the semiquaver triplet counterpoint to [15] taken by the soloist. From I/170, the characteristic rhythm and contour of this figure degenerate into arpeggio patterns in regular semiquaver triplets, leading to a codetta similar to that of the Scherzo. Many authorities follow Reich in reading this appearance of theme [8] as the beginning of a Scherzo reprise[8] – and indeed the cross-reference of material is clear – but the similarity of I/173 to I/132 is matched by the reminiscence of I/134 two bars later, and the parallelism is maintained as the harmonic progression into the Waltz (I/175–176) follows the pattern of I/135–136.

I/176–213 (Waltz) The waltz pastiche [20] is new, but its continuation [21] (I/180) draws the music back towards the material of the Scherzo. From I/188 the reprise is virtually exact, but with subtle changes which reinforce the waltz rhythm. The *rustico* is only lightly transformed, but the treatment of theme [14] at I/200 is in contrast to the earlier *tranquillo* interlude. No longer constrained by static harmony but instead supported by allusions to functional progressions (see pp. 72–5), the soloist's broad line builds forcefully, taking in developmental references to [8] (I/208) and [22] (I/210) as the music moves towards an interrupted (deceptive) cadence in G♭ major (I/213–14). Characteristically, this harmonically clearest of the form-defining cadences in the concerto – though cf. II/135–6 – follows the most evasive of traditional cadential schemata.

I/214–227 (Folk song) The increase in tension through the preceding section lends its release through the Carinthian folk song [23] an expressive focus that, together with the seemingly anomalous appearance of such a melody in this context, demands a programmatic interpretation. The song is presented more slowly than it might be sung, though its traditional yodelling *Überschlag* is preserved (I/218, solo violin); its accompaniment juxtaposes potentially functional triadic harmonies from the melody's G♭ major and the key most distant from it, C major – moving between these tonal orientations in a manner whose destabilising effect is itself counteracted by the rigour with which their rapid alternation is pursued.

I/228–257 (Coda) The music regains momentum with theme [19], whose countermelody (I/229, solo violin) is taken up by the woodwind at I/236 [24]; the *ritmico* brass figure from Trio I then powers the movement toward an inconclusive final cadence – the point of arrival being clearly delineated by means of phrasing and texture, but with a harmonic goal (Gm[7]) which, by comparison with many of the other harmonies exposed during the progress of Parts Ia and Ib, has no decisive connotation of tonal closure.

Movement IIa (Allegro)

II/...	material	length		
1–6	[25, 26]	6 bars	A	22 bars
7–14	[27, 27, 27]	8 bars		
15–22	[28, 25]	8 bars		
23–34	[29, 30]	12 bars	B	21 bars
35–43	[30]	9 bars		
44–53	[18]	10 bars	C	17 bars
54–60	[19, 31]	7 bars		
61–67	[32, 32]	7 bars	D	17 bars
68–77	[33, 32, 31]	10 bars		
78–90	[18]	13 bars	C'	18 bars
91–95	[19]	5 bars		
96–103	[25, 26]	8 bars	A'	40 bars
104–119	[30, 29, 30]	16 bars	(interpolation of B')	
120–124	[28, 25]	5 bars		
125–135	[34]	11 bars	(transition)	

II/1–22 (A) Gestures of improvisation dominate both solo and orchestral textures in this section. After an arpeggiated eight-note chord [25], the soloist adds the remaining four notes with an allusion to [1] (II/2), and then introduces a new theme [26] (II/4), comprising an angular ascent to a top D followed by a rushing descent to the lowest note of the instrument (see Example 11, p. 40). The extempore character of the music continues with [27] (II/7, cellos) and [28] (II/15, clarinets and saxophone), and while the underlying phrasing is quite strict and the section is rounded off by a return to the characteristic leaping figuration of [25] (II/19), the articulation of this rudimentary formal scheme is less striking than the quality of fragmentation inherent in the musical material.

II/23–43 (B) The marking *molto ritmico* introduces the *Hauptrhythmus* which is to dominate the rest of the Allegro [29],[9] while the soloist's music retains the improvisatory character previously established. The violin counterpoint at II/27 is reminiscent of theme [26], just as the bassoon and clarinet counterpoint at II/35 (where the violin takes over the repeating rhythmic figure) recalls [28]; the serial derivation of these melodic lines is obscure, suggesting perhaps that the improvisatory quality extended to the compositional process itself.[10] The music eventually settles at II/43 as the soloist introduces the incipit of the chorale in inversion.

II/44–60 (C) Theme [18], played at a slower tempo than before, is combined with the *Hauptrhythmus* (solo violin), the programmatic sense of the cross-reference to Part Ib being hinted at by the *dolente* marking which accompanies the descending chromatic pendant to the theme (II/50). Theme [19] also reappears (II/54–7) against a variant of [25], its improvisatory character now finding a more supportive context than in the earlier Trio, and the soloist introduces a new motive [31] at bar II/58 – though its shape has been foreshadowed at II/16–17 (solo violin) and II/17–18 (cellos).

II/61–77 (D) Bars II/61–5 [32] provide a model for the music of this section: a compositional improvisation on the inverted series followed by a development of [31] in which, at II/65 and II/67, it is combined with the chromatic motion of theme [18] using the cadenza-like technical device of left-hand pizzicato. At II/68–9 [33], the open strings of the work's opening bars support the whole-tone incipit of the chorale; then [31] is developed to a climax (II/73–4), after which its contour is liquidated (II/75–7, solo violin) as the music converges on the notes F, G♭ and E to recall [18].

II/78–95 (C') As the accompaniment drops away entirely, the soloist plays a four-part canon on theme [18]; the successive entries are at the distance of a perfect fifth, using the four strings of the instrument. Like the canonic and fugal writing in Bach's works for unaccompanied violin, the four-part counterpoint has to be suggested by skilful physical articulation of the three- and four-note chords which result. The realisation of the canon which Berg produced in consultation with Krasner reflects the then current manner of performing Bach's canons and fugues, and projects the four voices with less clarity than might now be thought desirable. Some violinists have reworked the canon in an effort to elucidate the contrapuntal structure for the listener;[11] others have followed Berg's alternative suggestion that the two upper voices be taken by the soloist and the two lower voices by the principal viola of the orchestra – solving the technical problem of the canon, but losing the characteristic Bergian paradox between the free spirit of the cadenza and the strictness of the counterpoint. At II/90, the canonic voices arrive at the four open strings of the instrument, recalling the opening of the concerto. This introduces a final recollection of the second Trio (II/91) in which the clarinets are once more introduced as a foil to the soloist's arco and pizzicato sonorities.

II/96–135 (A') A further variant of [25] builds up a twelve-note chord; the last to be added is a low F (II/97), which continues as a pedal point until the end of the movement. Theme [26] is now taken up by the violins of the orchestra as the twelve-note complex is split into two opposing diatonic planes: the sustained harmony in the woodwind and violas (II/99) and the headlong descent from the upper register (II/102–3) present the notes of C♭ major, while the soloist, in a figure recalling II/2, sounds the remaining notes, which sit diatonically with the pedal F.

A reprise of the *ritmico* music is interpolated (II/104), before an intensified repeat of the music of II/17–21 leads to an immense climax at II/125. The climactic material [34] comprises three elements: a dense chord played in the *Hauptrhythmus* – combining [25] and [29] – a leaping three-note melodic figure – distilled from [31] – and a whole-tone ascent – anticipating [35]. As the material is repeated through the ten bars which follow the explicitly marked *Höhepunkt* (climax), the leaping figure remains constant while the chord diminishes in both size and dynamic; the whole-tone ascent, on the other hand, develops from a single note to a four-note pattern, leading directly to the first phrase of the chorale. This melodic anticipation undermines the cadential effect arising from the 'resolution' of the pedal F to the B♭ major of the chorale quotation; at the same time, the interval repeatedly marked out by the violas in II/132–5 (E♭ to A) gels with the bass to suggest a functional F^7 chord; but this harmony is itself obscured by the unassimilable percussion and brass parts, barely audible though these are at the moment of transition.

Movement IIb (Adagio)

II/ ...	material	length		
136–146	[35, 35]	11 bars	Chorale	22 bars
147–151	[36, 36]	5 bars		
152–157	[37, 37, 37]	6 bars		
158–168	[35, 35]	11 bars	Variation 1	20 bars
169–174	[36, 36]	6 bars		
175–177	[37, 37]	3 bars		
178–189	[35i, 35i]	12 bars	Variation 2	22 bars
190–193	[36i, 36i]	4 bars		
194–199	[37i, 37i]	6 bars		
200–213	[23, 23]	14 bars	Folk song	14 bars
214–230	[35, 36, 37]	17 bars	Coda	17 bars

II/136–157 (Chorale) The chorale melody falls into three phrases [35], [36]

and [37], each of which is heard first in three-part counterpoint, based on the
twelve-note series (II/136, II/147, II/152, soloist, bassoon, lower strings),
and then in a generally homophonic tonal harmonisation adapted from Bach's
Cantata BWV 60 (1723) – played by a clarinet ensemble (again!) in imitation
of a small pipe organ (II/142, II/150, II/154). This treatment reflects the
repetitions that the original chorale melody by Johann Rudolf Ahle (1625–73)
employs in its setting of words by F.J. Burmeister, which are reproduced by
Berg in his score:

[35] Es ist genug! It is enough!
Herr, wenn es Dir gefällt, Lord, when it pleases Thee,
so spanne mich doch aus! Relieve me of my yoke!

[35] Mein Jesus kommt: My Jesus comes:
nun gute Nacht, o Welt! So goodnight now, O world!
Ich fahr' in's Himmelshaus. I'm going to my Heavenly home.

[36] Ich fahre sicher hin mit Frieden, I'll surely journey there in peace,

[36] mein großer Jammer bleibt darnieden.[12] My great distress will stay below.

[37] Es ist genug. It is enough.

[37] Es ist genug. It is enough.

The contrast of musical language arising from this direct quotation – a
contrast between Berg and Bach, rather than between tonality and atonality
– is maintained even during the quotation itself through the counterpoint of
a whole-tone motive played at II/143, II/145 and II/146–7 by the second
violins. This is itself derived from the opening of the chorale, however, and
the possibility of linguistic integration is raised further at II/155, where the
final phrase is echoed twice: the violin's serial treatment, using the inversion
on D, is now chordal rather than contrapuntal, and is intercut closely with
fragments of the Bach harmonisation.

II/158–177 (Variation 1) The phrases of the chorale melody are heard first
in E major (answered in canon at the fifth above by the harp) and then in B♭,
the two tonalities alternating just as the serial and Bachian treatments had
done previously. This alternation of tonalities recalls the orchestral interlude
(Variations) between the two scenes of Act III of *Lulu*, in which, according
to Reich's description, the diatonic theme is presented first in 'pure tonality'
(C major), then antiphonally in two keys (C major and G♭ major), then in a
setting in which tonality is 'completely dissolved', and finally within a serial
texture.[13] Here in the concerto, however, the alternation between tonalities a

tritone apart is slower – and therefore clearer – but also is accomplished through the series (see pp. 83–8). Thus the sense of motion towards a serial goal is denied in fact, even as it is raised in sound.

Contrapuntal interest is maintained within a richly harmonic texture through part-writing which is rhythmically freer than Bach's – a genuine bridge across the linguistic divide set up at I/136. In addition, at II/164, the solo violin introduces a substantial countermelody, the *Klagegesang* of Reich's programmatic account (see p. 33), which develops upwards towards the final phrase of the chorale (II/176). By the end of this variation, first one, then two, then half, and then all the first violins of the orchestra have joined the soloist in this plaint.

II/178–199 (Variation 2) In this second variation the melodic line is inverted, weakening its tonal orientation. The tritone alternation of phrase and repeated phrase continues, however, and a further imitation in the bass (II/185) takes the music to a climax in the next bar.[14] Although from II/184 onwards the musical texture arises almost entirely through the counterpoint of chorale statements and *Klagegesang*, the harmonic sense is paradoxically very strong: from II/189 to II/192 the bass settles on a pedal D, supporting a (much embellished) D^7 chord. But there is no local context to integrate this harmony within any larger tonal scheme – whether or not the occasional G minor references in Part I are still remembered.

After reaching its high point at II/186, played in octaves by all the upper strings of the orchestra, the elegy subsides, with the additional instruments gradually dropping out; eventually the soloist is alone again at II/196. The chorale melody also diminishes in dynamic: from II/198, as the soloist and bassoon recall the texture of II/136, the cellos repeat and develop the final phrase of the chorale towards the contour of the Carinthian folk melody.

II/200–213 (Folk song) Although the reappearance of the folk song begins on the second crotchet of II/200 (cellos), the transformation of the inverted last phrase of the chorale into its opening bar is as yet incomplete, so that the melody is recognisable only after it has begun.[15] The tempo is approximately twice as slow as in the Allegretto; otherwise the treatment is virtually identical, but the second phrase is taken by the violins of the orchestra rather than the trumpet, resulting in a more homogeneous texture that leads back towards the chorale model. The linking of two tonalities a tritone apart (here E♭ major and A major) continues the procedure of the first Chorale Variation, but the faster speed of alternation represents a development of this musical principle in the direction of fusion.

59

II/214–230 (Coda) This final section represents the closest confrontation yet with the possibility of linguistic integration, and its effect has divided critical opinion (see chapter 6). The chorale is presented by the full woodwind ensemble – a stronger sound than the earlier organ imitation, though reminiscent of it – in a texture which, like Bach's, is homophonic, but using serial harmony. At II/215, the soloist reintroduces the *Klagegesang*, leading it to a brief flourish (see below, p. 63) before taking up the final phrase of the chorale. From this point (the end of II/222), a succession of string soloists, rising from the double bass, presents the (also) rising contour of the concerto's series against repeated cadential statements of the chorale's final phrase in the brass – which conversely descend in pitch towards a whole-tone dominant-quality chord on G♭ (II/227).

The resolution of this chord, onto the tonic triad of B♭ with added sixth, follows a harmonic progression found frequently in 1930s dance-band arrangements; but, as so often before in this work, the cadential effect is simultaneously undermined, though not by the other voices in the texture. On the contrary, whereas elsewhere in the concerto a strong cadential articulation has tended to be contradicted in part by the musical material, here it is the rhythmic articulation which is indecisive, while the musical material denotes cyclic closure. The solo violin, taking over from the succession of orchestral string soloists, ascends to the added sixth (G) through the whole-tone motive from the chorale, while the 1st and 3rd horns descend through the inversion of this motive to the same note in a different octave. In the last two bars, even after the harmonic goal has been reached, the chord of the added sixth spreads upwards through the wind in a transformation of the opening material of the Allegro [25], while the orchestral strings recall the arpeggiated fifths which began the entire work [1].

A 'secret programme'?

Although the general nature of the concerto's orientation towards the programme of Manon Gropius's life, illness and release through death is clear enough, it is also plain that any attempt to interpret the detailed course of the music as narrative biography would be misguided. The musical discourse has a narrative quality of its own, and the credibility of its relation to an external programme does not rely on an unbroken parallelism, but rather on continual points of contact which sustain the illusion of unity between the music and the programme. The biographical programme itself must indeed be reckoned far from continuous: the prose account given by Reich on Berg's behalf (see pp. 32–3) is eclectic in its combination of references to the girl – either directly, or through words such as 'catastrophe', 'suffocating', 'cries for help', 'sad farewell' – and descriptions of the music; the weaving together of the two, as if to assert that their courses are bound together, is merely a device of language. This was not done to deceive, however, but in reflection of common practice: sufficient information is given for each listener to imagine both a musical and a dramatic continuity, and also to determine subjectively the interaction between the two.

The example of the once secret programme of the *Lyric Suite* complicates this, however, for in the annotated score which Berg gave to Hanna Fuchs the relation of the music to details of their private lives was so fully charted that it would be possible to regard the programmatic sense of the music as literally continuous.[16] And the relevance of this for the Violin Concerto in particular lies in the widespread appearance of Berg's private ciphers in the score of this work also: the numbers 10, 23 and 28 and the initials AB and HF. Douglas Jarman's investigation of this matter makes it clear that the origins of Berg's superstitions about the numbers 23 and 28 lay in his reading in 1914–15 of the work of Wilhelm Fliess, a biologist who, like many of his colleagues at the time, believed that numerological laws lie behind natural phenomena.[17] In Fliess's view, the number 23 was associated with men and 28 with women: it is not clear why Berg came to associate the number 10 with Hanna Fuchs, though it is clear that he did so.[18] The number 23 he associated with himself, partly in consequence of his having suffered a first asthma attack on 23 July 1908 (at the age of 23). In view of the fact that 28 plays no part in the numerology of the *Lyric Suite*, it would seem reasonable to read incidental appearances of the number 10 in the concerto as references to Hanna, and appearances of 28 as references to women in general, or to a woman other than Hanna. There is every reason to accept Jarman's view that the quotation of the Carinthian folk song should be read as an autobiographical reference to Berg's dalliance with Mizzi Scheuchl (see pp. 33–4),[19] and so it is possible that 28 might, in this work at least, be interpreted as 'her' number.

With no annotated score to guide such an interpretation, however, it is not always easy to identify numerological references and ciphers in the work with certainty. Still less is it possible to join them coherently into an alternative programme for the work, even though Willi Reich maintained as early as 1937 that there were 'secret relationships between the bar-numbers, just as in the Chamber Concerto'.[20] Just what sorts of data are to be considered? The examples of the Chamber Concerto and the *Lyric Suite* suggest ciphers of both initials of personal names – *A*lban *B*erg, *H*anna *F*uchs – and letter names of pitches *within* personal names – *ArnolD SCHönBErG*, *A*nton w*EBE*rn, *A*l*BA*n *BE*r*G*; numbers appear principally as lengths of sections (counted in bars) or in metronome markings. The letters available are those which have musical equivalents in German, i.e. A, B (B♭), C, D, E, F, G, H (B♮) and S ('Es', i.e. E♭);[21] numbers may appear straightforwardly, or as multiples (e.g. $69 = 23 \times 3$), or possibly through addition, multiplication (etc.) of digits (e.g. $5 = 2 + 3$, $10 = 2 + 8$).[22] Jarman lists a considerable number of plausible examples, particularly in the Chorale Variations:

- the metronome markings of Parts I and II are multiples of 28 and 23 respectively (movement IIb departs from this pattern)

- Part II has 230 bars ($= 23 \times 10$)

- the *Hauptrhythmus* is first heard at bar II/23

- bars I/1–10 are marked explicitly as 'Introduction (10 bars)'

- the reprise in the Andante is at bar I/84 ($= 28 \times 3$)

- B♭–A–G–E (cf. *A*l*BA*n *BE*r*G*) is outlined in the 23rd bar of movement IIb (first horn)

- the *Höhepunkt* of the Adagio is at the 23rd bar of the *Klagegesang*

- HF occurs in the solo part at the 23rd bar after the second folk song quotation (i.e. II/222)

In addition, Jarman shows how distances of 23 (actually 22) or 28 bars, or multiples of 10 bars, divide important moments across the whole of the Adagio, and quotes numerical calculations found in the margins of Berg's sketches for the latter part of movement Ib.[23]

Further consideration of the lengths of sections within the entire work throws up other correspondences. Movement Ia is 103 bars in length, Ib is 154: from Trio II to the end of the movement, however, is also 103 bars, dividing Part I into 103, 51 and 103 bars all told: the 51-bar section is itself divided into 28 + 23 bars by the reappearance of the first Scherzo theme [8]. Part II is similarly divided, but in mirror fashion: the Allegro has 135 bars, the Adagio 95, with the reprise of the Allegro coming at II/96 and so dividing Part II into 95, 40 and 95 bars. Moreover, the reappearance of the *Hauptrhythmus* at II/104 marks the end of a 103-bar segment which thus links the proportional organisation of Parts I and II together. But it is not at all clear what these numbers might 'mean' programmatically, particularly 103 and 95. Within the Andante, the 10 + 10 + 7 phrasing of the beginning returns in retrograde at the retransition; the material between the two A sections covers 46 (i.e. 23 × 2) bars. In the Allegretto, the third appearance of theme [8], at I/173, comes after 69 (i.e. 23 × 3) bars: this is marked in the score by a double bar-line.[24] Appearances of Berg's fateful numbers are not difficult to drum up: Part I has 257 bars, i.e. (28 × 10) − 23; the two folk song sections total 28 bars, and the remainder of the music totals 243 bars in Part I, i.e. 3 to the power (2 + 3), and 216 bars in Part II, i.e. (2 × 3) to the power 3.[25] Nor is it difficult to find places where smaller phrases may be grouped together into units of 46 and 56 bars. But the easier it is to find such things, the less significant they become, unless supported by other kinds of knowledge about their possible programmatic function.

As well as the 'confessional' folk song, certain expression markings attached to the phrases of the chorale melody on each and every occurrence have been interpreted as references to a secret programme of some kind. The three parts of [35] are always marked *deciso*, *doloroso* and *dolce*; [36] carries the marking *risoluto* and [37] is *molto espressivo e amoroso*; the 'amoroso' in particular has suggested a connection with Hanna Fuchs.[26] The final appearance of this phrase (II/222) is preceded by a flourish on the solo violin which emphasises the ABFH cell so prominent in the *Lyric Suite*,[27] and Jarman has suggested that the end of the concerto carried a message to Hanna along the lines of Geschwitz's dying promise to Lulu of eternal union in the hereafter.[28] This would seem to depend, first of all, on reading the tragedy as Berg's tragedy, perhaps simultaneously with Manon's – but then this is a view which has long been part of the folklore surrounding the concerto.[29] Serious consideration of the idea has been hindered by the hagiographic quality it inevitably acquired in view of the composer's almost immediate death, but it is clear that an autobiographical sequence would have 'made sense' in any case, being so close in its broad outline to the 'official' biographical programme concerning the tragedy of Alma Mahler's daughter.[30]

Whether the listener conceives this alternative programme in sufficient detail to include, for example, an interpretation of the first 'groaning' *ritmico* at II/23 as a reference to Berg's first attack of asthma, is not of fundamental importance. The discontinuous nature of the programmatic interactions between music and narrative makes the details of such interpretations a matter of individual taste and response. On the other hand, the discovery of a precise musical reference for the extraordinary – yet also musically appropriate – expression markings in the chorale, along the lines of Alwa's reference via the *Lyric Suite* to Hanna in the Hymne of Act II scene 2 of *Lulu*,[31] would make an important contribution to those developing interpretations, just as

Jarman's apparent solution of the jigsaw-puzzle of numerology, folk song and youthful indiscretion has done. The nature of his work also demonstrates that watertight scholarship alone is not enough: for although numerological 'analysis' of musical works is a minefield – it is perhaps a blessing that Berg comfortably missed the Golden Section in his divisions of both Parts I and II – there is no doubt of its potential relevance to an understanding of Berg's intentions. And in so far as the listener's programmatic interpretation of the work depends upon the possibly illusory reassurance that the composer's intentions have indeed been understood, then such discussion will surely continue.

Harmony, tonality and the series

Tonal or atonal?

Writing in 1949 of his Second String Quartet (1907–8), whose fourth movement is frequently cited as an early example of 'atonality', Schoenberg outlined the dilemma which this music exposed through its interactions of counterpoint, harmony and form:

... there are many sections in which the individual parts proceed regardless of whether their meeting results in codified harmonies. Still, here, and also in the third and fourth movements, the key is distinctly present at all the main dividing-points of the formal organization. Yet the overwhelming multitude of dissonances cannot be counterbalanced any longer by occasional returns to such tonic triads as represent a key. It seemed inadequate to force a movement into the Procrustean bed of a tonality without supporting it by harmonic progressions that pertain to it.[1]

For Schoenberg, the difficulty was only to be answered by the renunciation of tonal centres – a 'decisive step' which he took immediately in the songs Op. 14 and Op. 15 and the Piano Pieces Op. 11. It was this renunciation which others – wrongly, he thought – characterised as 'atonality'.

Berg's Violin Concerto cannot be regarded as 'atonal' in these terms, for there is no evidence in it that tonal centres have been renounced; on the contrary, the returns to triadic formations at points of formal articulation appear to conform exactly to the terms of Schoenberg's discussion. As described by Douglas Jarman, Part I is centred on G minor, in the sense that either this key or one of its close relatives is identifiable as a tonal centre at a number of formally or thematically important junctures:

I/11	a tempo	G minor
I/84	Tempo I	G minor
I/104	Allegretto	D minor
I/114	*rustico*	B♭ major
I/132	Tempo I	D minor

I/155	Trio II	G major/minor
I/173	Quasi Tempo I	D minor
I/257	[final bar]	G minor[2]

Along with many other recognised aspects of the work's musical language, this cannot be explained merely by tracing the derivation of the music from the series – the natural first response of a score-reading analyst. One can hardly deny the force of this reading, however, which may easily be extended to Part II. Here, the long pedal F and the B♭ tonality of the chorale, together with the reappearance of the Carinthian folk song in E♭ major, may be understood to project B♭ major as the overall tonal orientation.

As Schoenberg's essay points out, however, it is difficult to reconcile these occasional references to tonal centres with the general absence of such harmonic progressions and other moment-by-moment musical details as would normally be expected to support them. Organic tonality of the kind Schoenberg evoked here was to form the basis for the structuralist analysis of tonal music along Schenkerian lines, an approach which became widely respected in the three decades that followed his essay. But this model of tonality was rarely applied to music which alluded only occasionally to the harmonic and linear norms of the eighteenth and nineteenth centuries, because it was difficult to construct an integrated reading in these circumstances. The tensions that were likely to arise were indicated in a methodological statement by the Schenkerian theorist James Baker:

Under no circumstances does the mere pointing out of tonal-like configurations, gestures or progressions constitute a valid analysis establishing the tonality of a composition. Rather, in order to demonstrate that such components fulfill tonal functions, their precise roles within a conventional hierarchical tonal structure must always be specified. If no such explanation is possible, a basis in another type of structure must be sought.[3]

According to neo-Schenkerian theory, then, Berg's concerto is not 'tonal', either, because the identification of tonal centres at certain moments is not sufficient to establish a hierarchical tonal structure.

The structuralist alternative advocated by Baker and others was Allen Forte's theory of atonal music – though in reality it is the theory itself which is 'atonal', in the sense that it excludes tonal terminology.[4] A full account of Forte's approach is neither necessary nor possible here, but in essence it has two components: (i) an exhaustive categorisation of all possible collections of equally tempered pitches, so that no chord or motivic fragment, however unusual, should resist systematic classification; and (ii) a way of analysing individual pieces which finds significance in the recurrence of related groupings. The way in which this relatedness is predetermined by the system of categorisation is therefore crucial. Forte's system is reductive, distilling similarity out of different pitch configurations – from which all aspects of rhythm, instrumentation and dynamics are assumed already to have been removed – according to the following principles:

- the registers in which the pitches appear are disregarded

- enharmonically related pitches are regarded as equivalent

This places each pitch into one of twelve *pitch-classes* corresponding to the twelve notes within the octave, which are numbered chromatically upwards from 0 (C♮) to 11 (B♮). The myriad of possible ordered or unordered collections (*sets*) of from one to twelve pitch-classes is then brought within manageable proportions by further systematic reduction:

- the order in which the pitch-classes occur is disregarded

- sets which are transpositionally related (irrespective of pitch-class order) are regarded as equivalent

- sets which are inversionally related are similarly regarded as equivalent

Taking sets of, for example, three pitch-classes, this reduces the 1,320 possible collections to just twelve types of set (*set-classes*), numbered 3–1, 3–2 . . . 3–12; the 665,280 possible hexachords are similarly reduced to fifty (6–1, etc.). Although the whole procedure may at first sight appear crude and calculating, it has promoted valuable insights into some difficult music from the early twentieth century.[5] It is certainly an approach which can draw similarities between musical textures that at first sight look very different: Example 12 analyses two passages from Berg's concerto in this way, indicating that set-classes 4–19, 5–34 and 7–34 recur across them. (The similarity of numbering between 5–34 and 7–34 indicates that these set-classes are 'complementary' – another important element of the theory. It means, for example, that for each set of type 5–34 there is another of type 7–34 which is made up of precisely those pitch-classes omitted from the smaller set.)[6]

Using the standard notation for identifying transpositions of prime and inverse serial forms – with P_0, for example, meaning the prime form that begins on pitch-class 0 (C♮) – this example also indicates the derivations of these passages from the series. And, as the correlation between these modes of analysis serves to show, the principles behind Forte's classification of pitch-

Example 12. Serial forms and pitch-class sets in (a) I/104–5; (b) I/114–5

class sets are in fact almost entirely cognate with the principles of serial composition established by Schoenberg:

- the series does not predetermine the registral position of any note

- the series does not determine the enharmonic spelling of any note

- the series may be transposed and inverted freely

inevitably, complementary sets will arise whenever a twelve-note serial statement is split into two adjacent segments

While the central question of order remains, it will be seen that, to the extent that the notes are grouped together – as in the analyses of Example 12 – their precise serial order is obliterated. Thus, like any work which adheres in a general way to the twelve-note technique, the Violin Concerto undoubtedly has a Fortean 'atonal structure' which one might determine through analysis; but, equally, its serial basis removes any necessity for such detailed 'proof' that the music is atonal in these terms. The broader limitations of the approach are thrown into relief by a work such as this, whose acknowledged richness disdains the essentially hermetic structures determined by Fortean methods, just as surely as it demands far more from the analyst than the obligatory charting of serial derivations. While the very different interpretative route through which the recognition of tonal centres comes about is admittedly difficult to trace, it is more important to keep faith with such recognitions than to force one's interpretation into a Procrustean bed of either the tonal or the atonal kind.

Extensions of tonality

If neither the accepted structural definition of tonality nor that of atonality seems applicable to the concerto, it must be asked just how one should attempt to present the details of a musical understanding which goes beyond the occasional recognition of tonal centres. Although these recognitions cannot be integrated into a fully Schenkerian view, other conceptions of tonality are of course possible: Schoenberg himself did not subscribe to Schenker's theories, although his principle of 'monotonality' also emphasised integration.[7] In explaining this principle, he discussed the relationships between harmonic progressions, modulations and the establishment of tonalities in terms of 'centrifugal' and 'centripetal' tendencies, and this idea was later given a historical dimension by Carl Dahlhaus, who associated the first with Wagner and the second with Brahms.[8] It could be argued that Schoenberg's tendency in his later years to align himself with a Brahmsian conception of tonality was part of his wish to be seen as a traditionalist – though the complex ambivalence of his thought is as fully reflected in his technical writings as it is in his compositions. At any rate, one may readily accept Dahlhaus's suggestion that another of Schoenberg's technical concepts, that of 'floating' tonality, is more appropriate to Wagner's music.[9] This originated in Schoenberg's pre-war *Harmonielehre*,[10] and in the present context it should be recalled that Berg's seminal period of rigorous self-appraisal in 1913 came in the wake both of his work on the index to this treatise and of his preparation of the piano score of Schoenberg's most obviously Wagnerian work, the *Gurrelieder* (see pp. 10, 20). It is by no means immediately apparent that the term may be applied to Berg's own works, however, and indeed the pattern of key-references identified by Jarman in the Violin Concerto is remarkably uniform, if not 'unified'. What is left out of consideration in this analysis is a close description of the moment-by-moment progress of the music, and an assessment of how it might support the reading of a large-scale tonal orientation.

Schoenberg himself was not able to supply a close description of what he meant by 'floating tonality', but he cited the Prelude to Wagner's *Tristan* as an example:

[A minor], although it is to be inferred from every passage, is scarcely ever sounded in the whole piece. It is always expressed in circuitous ways; it is constantly avoided by means of deceptive cadences.[11]

Neither specific examples nor a unified terminology, it seemed, were adequate to describe the phenomenon, though it was clear that 'rich resources must be at hand to bring it about.' Among these resources were the ambiguous 'vagrant' chords, such as the diminished seventh chord, which could potentially be heard as functional in a number of tonalities, and hence had 'multiple meaning'. Harmonic progressions in which such chords were prominent he described as 'roving', and passages of roving harmony he saw as characteristic of floating tonality:

Roving harmony is based on multiple meaning. Accordingly chords which are vagrants because of their constitution are very effective for this purpose: diminished 7th chords, augmented triads, augmented 6–5 and 4–3 chords, Neapolitan triads, other transformations and . . . [chords composed of fourths].[12]

At the same time:

Roving harmony need not contain extravagant chords. Even simple triads and dominant 7th chords may fail to express a tonality.[13]

But floating tonality was only one of a number of possibilities. A more extreme case was 'suspended tonality':

The purely harmonic aspect will involve almost exclusive use of explicitly vagrant chords [because any] major or minor triad could be interpreted as a key, even if only in passing.[14]

In the light of Schoenberg's remarks about his Second String Quartet (see p.

65), it would seem that it was just such a suspension of tonality, through the final exclusion of tonal centres, that came to be regarded as 'atonality' by his critics.

This was certainly Berg's answer when faced in 1930 with the question 'What is Atonality?'[15] He maintained that the word had originated in order to denote the helplessness felt by listeners who could not follow the 'harmonic course' of music which did not conform to the previously recognised 'laws of tonality'. At the same time, he argued that the 'new chord-forms' arising from the chromatic scale could articulate a harmonic centre, albeit differently, and devoted the major part of his response to technical matters of harmony, melody, rhythm, form and counterpoint. He argued that melody, even in Schubert, was constrained by harmony, and stated that this was the case with his 'atonal' melodies also. Similarly, in an article he had written six years earlier on the musical language of Schoenberg's First String Quartet (1904–5), he had drawn a harmonic 'skeleton' of the opening of the work, in order to show how its angular contrapuntal textures were based on a succession of chords which would 'be immediately clear to any ear educated in the harmony of the [nineteenth] century.'[16] Berg's insistence on a continuity of practice – from the nineteenth century through Schoenberg's Quartet to his own more recent music – was in accordance with Schoenberg's analysis of the origins of the new chord-types in the *Harmonielehre*. Schoenberg had argued that new chords arose through the chromatic alteration of old ones, from the diatonic church modes or the whole-tone scale, or were built in fourths (rather than the more conventional thirds). And while this formulation doubtless reflected an ideological desire to emphasise links with the past, it also observed the technical connection between harmony and melody through its explicit consideration of chromatic, diatonic and other linear resources.

Berg's idea that listeners might be unable to follow the harmonic course of a piece of music, and Schoenberg's suggestion that a triad could be interpreted as a momentary reference to a key, are similar in their focus on the moment-by-moment recognition of tonal centres rather than larger tonal orientations. But a further remark of Schoenberg's seems to lead beyond his descriptions of suspended tonality and floating tonality, finding a new accommodation for broadly spaced tonal references:

Extended tonality may contain roving segments, though, on the other hand, various regions may occasionally be firmly established.[17]

In view of the clearly recognisable tonal centres in the Violin Concerto, this description would seem to lay the basis for a wide-ranging analysis of the work

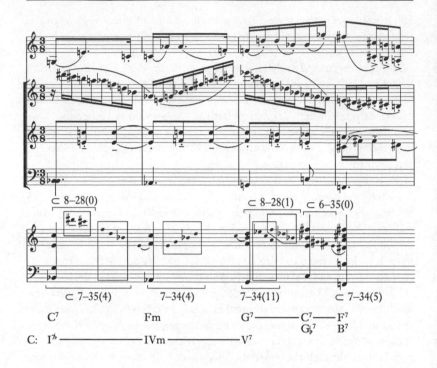

Example 13. I/200–7 (cont. on p. 73)

on both the large and the small scale. But, like the suspended and floating varieties, what this concept of 'extended tonality' does not provide is a systematic means for the structural analysis of this work or any other. Schoenberg's admitted inability to supply any models in the *Harmonielehre* for imitation by readers was a symptom, however, not a failing. His apparently despairing exhortation to study the examples he cites from his own compositions – 'if one takes a look at them, one will know what I mean' – is a precise statement of the central role of recognition in musical understanding.[18] In this context, the role of analysis is to show how such recognitions may be made via a range of models, comprising linear resources, individual harmonic types, schematic progressions, and perhaps other things besides. Just how the tonality is 'extended' will be seen from the particular models invoked, and from the ways in which they interact in the interpretation of specific musical passages.

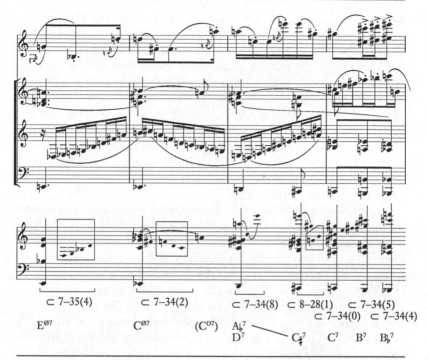

Key to set-classes in Example 13:	measured upwards in semitones against
7–35 diatonic major scale, descending minor scale	the recognised standard forms:
7–34 ascending minor scale, V¹³ (in major)	7–35(0) = D♭ major, B♭ minor
8–28 octatonic scale	7–34(0) = C♯ minor, F♯¹³ (in B major)
6–35 whole-tone scale	8–28(0) = C, D♭, E♭, E, F♯, G, A, B♭
Numbers in parentheses indicate transpositions,	6–35(0) = C, D, E, F♯, A♭, B♭

'Rich resources must be at hand'

Both Schoenberg's theoretical writings and Berg's 'harmonic skeleton' indicate that they saw many of the newer types of chord, such as the [0,3,6,10] half-diminished seventh[19] and various chords of the ninth and thirteenth, as less rigidly 'functional' than the major and minor triads and 6–5 chords. That is to say, these chords could be incorporated, through diatonic or chromatic voice-leading, within a wide variety of musical contexts, and any one such chord could lead to any other. On the other hand, the cadential quality which had originated with the [0,4,7,10] dominant seventh chord could now apply to the [0,3,6,9] diminished seventh and to four- or five-note chords built in fourths, as well as to various whole-tone chords, from the [0,4,8] augmented triad and the [0,4,10] outline of the dominant seventh to the complete [0,2,4,6,8,10] whole-tone aggregate. In particular, the expansion of the [0,4,10] model by the addition of the note a tritone from the root, creating an [0,4,6,10] sonority, had the effect of combining the original [0,4,10] with its tritone transposition [6,10,4], drawing the associated diatonic scales into a 'vagrant' harmonic complex. This, through allusion to the larger tertiary structures of the ninth and thirteenth, could in a twelve-note context give a qualitative tonal orientation to any pitch by reference to one or other (or both) of the tritone-related tonal centres. In a B^7/F^7 complex, for example, a $C^\sharp$ might have the quality of the perfect fifth degree (in relation to F) and/or the minor ninth (in relation to B).

A summary of bars I/200–7 of the Violin Concerto (Example 13) illustrates the music's affinity with extended tonal resources of various kinds. The first three chords (bars I/200–2) follow a well-established schema of harmonic progression (I^7–IVm–V^7); the continuation (G^7–C^7–F^7) also conforms to a familiar pattern of dominant-quality chords following a root progression by ascending fourths, while the tendency for tritone-related elements to accumulate increases towards the end of the phrase. The second four-bar phrase begins with two half-diminished sevenths – taking the violin's G, rather than the orchestra's A, as a harmony note in I/204 – and after the second of these has moved to a diminished seventh by chromatic motion in one part, the harmony comprises a succession of dominant-quality chords following a root progression by semitonal descent (I/206–7). After this, the music continues through root progression upwards by a fourth onto a whole-tone expansion of the compound dominant on E♭ and A (I/208), and the rest of the phrase consists of dominant-quality chords connected by semitonal or ascending-fourth root progressions. Finally, the Carinthian folk song is reached at I/214 through a V–VI ('interrupted' or 'deceptive') cadence into G♭ major.

As this analysis also indicates, the contrapuntal motion within the duration of each chord may frequently be aligned with an established linear resource, such as the diatonic scale, the dominant-quality [0,2,4,6,7,9,10] 'acoustic' scale, the whole-tone scale or the [0,1,3,4,6,7,9,10] octatonic scale of alternating semitones and whole tones.[20] The interaction of harmonic and linear resources in a complex musical texture can signal the passing orientation of a chord to a tonal centre – cf. the appoggiaturas at I/22 (Example 14) which project the D♭ major triad momentarily as VI in F minor – and the web of potential relationships among the range of tonal resources outlined here allows

74

Example 14. I/20–2

a rich play of alternatives. The analysis of I/200–3 indicates that even schemata of functional harmonic progression are recognisable, and a comparison between I/202–3 and I/206–7 illustrates how the 'applied dominant' root progression by ascending fourth may be correlated with a parallel semitonal descent of dominant-quality chords through the tritone substitution which was routine in 1930s jazz harmony – seen in outline at I/20–1 (Example 14).

A tritone link between tonal orientations is also to be observed in connection with the musical *objets trouvés* in the concerto, both in the (non-serial) harmonic treatment of the Carinthian folk song and as a technique of thematic variation in the (serial) Chorale Variations in Part IIb (see pp. 83–8). In the folk song harmonisation, the linear resources of the whole-tone and octatonic scales are drawn into a constant alternation of chords paired at the tritone, as are allusions to tonic, dominant and subdominant harmonic functions. This is illustrated more concisely at I/134 (Example 15): the octatonic conjunction of tritone-related major triads at I/134–5 forms a dominant-quality complex which 'resolves' by ascending fourth onto another such complex around F and B major triads, while in I/136, the simultaneous scalar motions within these triads are in alignment with a single whole-tone scale.

Example 15. I/134–7

The series

What is the role of the series in all this? Schoenberg argued that in suspended tonality 'the theme is undoubtedly the crux of the matter',[21] as its linearity could supply a coherence that the constantly roving harmony lacked. And, since a twelve-note series is, axiomatically, a linear entity, it is clear that it too has the capacity to supply a thread on which a succession of shifting harmonies may be strung. It is not, however, explicitly thematic, nor can its blindly logical principle of coherence – the exhaustion of all twelve pitch-classes – have been in Schoenberg's mind at the time when he wrote the *Harmonielehre*. One might therefore suppose that the linear coherence of a series, in the context of suspended tonality, should be perceived through its

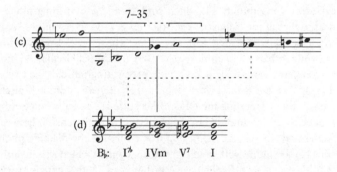

Example 16

tonalistic orientation, as in the *Lyric Suite* and *Lulu*, where Berg employed series which fall cleanly into two halves that lie within diatonic scales a tritone apart (see pp. 18–19, 22). As has been seen above, this tritone link is integral to the extended tonality of the Violin Concerto – perhaps even more so than the much vaunted triadic structure of the work's series – and it is seen in a twelve-note context in the climactic separation of C♭ major and F major pitches at II/99–103.

Although the series itself does not share this tonalistic property, its first seven notes correspond to an ascending 'melodic' minor scale, reordered as a chain of thirds (Example 16a): in the form most frequently quoted (P₇) the

Example 17

scalar allegiance is to G minor. The pitch content of these opening notes is also identical to that of the 'acoustic' scale (set-class 7–34, *cf.* Example 12, p. 68); the minor modality is shared with *Der Wein*, whose series begins with a complete ascending 'harmonic' minor scale. Berg's habitual circular rotation of the series (so that one may begin anywhere, proceeding through the twelve notes as through the hours on a clock) means that the two additional pitch-classes found in the descending melodic minor scale are actually adjacent to this seven-note group (Example 16b). Considering the relationship between the same series and the relative major (B♭) it is clear that the diatonic pitch-classes of this key are found within an eight-note segment which also includes pitch-class 6 (Example 16c). Spelled as G♭ rather than F♯, this note is crucial to the routine harmonic schema exemplified at bars I/200–2 of the concerto, as the minor third of the IVm triad (Example 16d).

Bars I/200–3 (Example 13, pp. 72–3) illustrate further how the tritone link is involved in the alignment of the concerto's series with the chromatic expansion of diatonic scalar resources. While the serial structure of this passage is of a characteristic complexity, it is clear that a principal thread in the fabric of interwoven serial statements is to be found in the solo violin part. As shown in Example 17a, this follows the series at I₇ with only the note D♯ omitted (it is played by the orchestra). This form of the series is the rotated retrograde of P₃ (Example 17b) which, in correspondence with the allegiance of P₇ to B♭ major, suggests G♭; yet the analysis of the harmonic schemata underlying this passage has suggested C major, a tritone away. In fact, the series is equivalently aligned with the extended diatonic resources representative of both tonalities: the ten-note segments bracketed in Example 17b contain the same scale degrees, a tritone apart. Rather than falling into two tritone-related halves, therefore, the series achieves a cross-fade between each tonality and its tritone twin. The compound dominant chords in I/202–3 arise through the counterpoint between serial motion through this tritone in the solo part and a tonally stable harmonic schema in the orchestra; similarly, in the principal material of the Allegretto (I/103, see Example 12, p. 68), the bass remains rooted on D while the upper parts move, outlining the complementary seventh chord (A♭, C, E♭, G♭) at the end of the bar.

The four-note cell whose duplication at the tritone is highlighted by open notes in Example 17b has a particular significance in this context. Stated melodically, this cell begins the Carinthian folk tune; as a simultaneity, it ends the work as Schoenberg's *Gurrelieder* begins, with the chord of the added sixth. This expansion of the major triad, familiar in light music of the 1930s, is technically akin to the expansion of the diatonic scale as a melodic resource, but its appearance at the end of the concerto is typically Bergian in the way it encompasses stylistic allusion – to popular music as much as to the last page of *Das Lied von der Erde* – while fulfilling a cadential function demonstrably in line with the larger resources explored during the course of the work.[22]

Serial working

The analyses of thematic and motivic material seen so far illustrate the Schoenbergian function of the series, as a *Grundgestalt* which, in an essentially intangible way, binds together not only all the thematic material of the work (with the exception of the *objets trouvés*)[23] but also underlies the other contrapuntal and harmonic elements of its textures. At the same time, the listener does not perceive such harmony and counterpoint in terms of its serial basis but instead with reference to more familiar models. It is through this process that the music of the concerto may be understood in the context of a wider repertoire. As has been outlined in chapter 3 (see p. 31), Berg's sketches show how he himself sought ways both to isolate scalar units from the series (Example 18a; see also Example 9a, p. 38) and to derive from it chord progressions which could be encompassed by conventional harmonic theory. On the sketch sheet headed 'Chords and Cadences', he designated chords by scale degrees such as I and V (Examples 18b–e), and also isolated the famous overlapping triads within the row in both prime and inverse forms (Examples

Example 18. Adapted from ÖNB Musiksammlung,
F 21 Berg 85/I, fol. 8 (a) and fol. 6 (b–g)

18f–g). The first of these (transposed to P_7) is the basis of bars I/11–14; the second follows the conventional schema of root progression by descending fifths (equivalent to ascending fourths) and appears at I_1 in the *ritmico* material (I/140).[24]

The peculiarly Bergian aspects of serial technique in *Lulu*, as identified by Willi Reich and George Perle, include the following:[25]

- various series are derived from the basic series by systematic procedures

- a series may be defined not exclusively by the order of its notes, but rather by its segmental pitch-class content

- a series may be associated with a melodic contour, over and above its function as a register-independent determinant of pitch-class succession

- the perceptibility of such contours in inversion, and the difficulty of perceiving them in retrograde, leads to the virtual exclusion of retrograde and retrograde-inversion serial forms from the music

These principles do not entirely hold in the Violin Concerto, however. Perhaps the most important difference is the lack of subsidiary series, of which *Lulu* has more than a dozen: the composition history of the opera makes it plain, however, that Berg began to use derived series only when the difficulty of extracting new material from the original single series became an obstacle to his powers of invention. This problem simply did not arise in the case of the Violin Concerto, where the process of composition outlined in chapter 3 (pp. 29–30) generated sufficient thematic material for the entire work. On the other hand, the second principle – that of segmental pitch content taking priority over strict ordering – is carried over to some extent from the opera into the concerto through the accommodation of the series to conventional harmonic models. Through both the triadic voicing of the first part of the series and the disposition of the concluding whole-tone segment as a dominant ninth, as at I/162, the precise order of the notes is subordinated to a group identity; and another feature of the serial writing – amounting in this case to a genuine reordering – is the frequent disposition of the whole-tone group as two major thirds, as at I/155 (cellos), II/1 (upper parts), II/75 (C/E, D/F$\sharp$), II/93 (soloist) and II/98–9 (violins). The melodic contour of the concerto's series is essentially unidirectional, in contrast to the balanced rise and fall shown by most of the series in *Lulu*, but an alternative zigzagging contour, first explored at I/47, assumes prominence in Part II. It is not the perceptibility of contour that causes the exclusion of retrograde and retrograde-inversion forms from the concerto, however, since the retrograde is simply a rotation of the inversion (*cf.* Example 17, p. 78). On the other hand, Berg's sketches indicate that, while recognising this fact, he did not entirely exclude the retrograde and retrograde-inversion forms from his conception. A specific example is the *Klagegesang* (II/164), which he derived from the retrograde-inversion and prime forms of the series (Example 19).

This is not the only passage where notes are taken in alternation from two or more serial forms – others include the solo part at I/81–3,[26] I/145–7, II/5–7, II/22, II/54–5 and II/73–6. The results range from the grace-note groups of I/81 and II/54 to the scalar writing of II/5, II/22 and II/164; from the measured appoggiaturas of II/178 to the improvisatory quality of I/145, II/73, II/184 and II/190.[27] An exactly opposite procedure is found in the first ten bars of the work, where alternate notes are extracted from the series, producing the 'open strings' motive. Both these techniques are characteristic of Berg, not simply in their subordination of the strict dodecaphonic basis to the production of conventional musical figurations, but also in achieving this apparent freedom through a higher serial complexity. At the same time, the

Example 19. Serial origin of *Klagegesang* (adapted from
ÖNB Musiksammlung, F 21 Berg 85/II, fol. 3v)

treatment of the Trio II material is no less characteristic in its relegation of
serial technique to the status of a prop. Though sketched directly from the
series (see pp. 37–8), this derivation is disguised even on the music's first
appearance at I/155; it is further obscured on its reminiscence at II/44, and
totally dispensed with in the four-part canon at II/78.

A third way of working with the series is even more radical in its departure
from both the spirit and the letter of Schoenbergian orthodoxy. This is to be
found in the developmental continuation of themes, in the treatment of the
chorale melody, and in other circumstances where the essential compositional
objective seems to have been the accommodation of some preconceived
musical pattern into a serial context. In effect, the series in such passages is
functionally partitioned: those notes belonging to the preconceived object are
deployed to produce it, while the remainder are placed in the texture in a
manner which pays scant respect to their serial order, but on the contrary

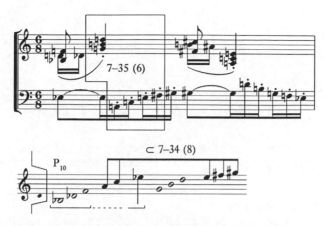

Example 20. I/137 (cf. ÖNB Musiksammlung, F 21 Berg 85/II, fol. 26v)

seems calculated as an exercise in damage limitation, preserving the extended tonal language as far as possible. It is a measure of Berg's technical mastery that such passages rarely betray to the ear the contrivance that attempts at serial analysis will reveal.[28]

The material of the Trio I section of Part Ib illustrates some of these principles (Example 20). Sketched originally a semitone lower, but otherwise essentially as it appears in the final score, this material seems to originate in the extraction of two triads (B♭ minor, G major) from the series at P_{10}. But the remaining pitches are themselves edited, so that the E♭, which sits diatonically with the B♭ triad, appears out of sequence, while the rest of the notes support the G major triad – indeed these pitches all lie within the 'acoustic' scale associated with the dominant of G major. The ensuing phrase proceeds by alternating prime and inverse forms of this material, with the sustained bass notes following a progression by ascending fourths, notated enharmonically.

The first Chorale Variation

A more extended passage in which serial pitches are accommodated to pre-existing material within an extended tonal framework is the first Chorale Variation (II/158–77). This falls into three phrases, in line with the alternating phrases of the chorale melody: in II/158–63 the first six bars of the chorale are heard in E major (cellos); the same phrase is heard in B♭ major

Example 21. II/158–64 (cont. on p. 85)

in II/164–9 (trombone). The subsequent phrases are shorter and are thus exchanged more rapidly in the next eight bars (II/170–7), but still in these two keys.

Example 21 shows how the music of II/158–63 may be heard in alignment with various extended tonal resources. In correspondence with the written nuances of tempo, indicating points of cadential articulation at the beginning and end of this section, it is at these points that the harmonic associations are the strongest. The opening chord (I/158) is a dominant-quality octatonic sonority on E, melded with B♭; the harmony of II/163 at first suggests the dominant of E major, moving on the third beat to an Em⁶⁻⁵ chord which resolves in accordance with a familiar tonal schema to a V⁷ chord in B minor. Between these points the vertical sonorities conform less clearly to familiar harmonic archetypes, but lie nevertheless within diatonic or other familiar scalar collections.

There is a gradual shift through bars II/158–9 from the octatonic collection [1,2,4,5,7,8,10,11] to the diatonic collection [0,1,3,5,7,8,10]. This progression is initiated on the second crotchet of II/158 by the textural articulation of a B♭ minor triad, and cued on the next downbeat by a B♭ minor triad in root position (with major seventh), but it is not completed until the A♮ gives way to A♭ on the fourth beat of II/159. At the same time, the linear motion in the bass follows the 'acoustic' scale associated with E⁷, falling out of alignment precisely as the harmonic gamut settles on the diatonic set. (This motion through 7–34 within an octatonic area, and other instances of tonally coordinated modal interaction, are indicated in Example 21 by enclosures around the linear motions concerned.) Further points of interest include the dominant-quality chord on the last beat of II/161, whose cadential association is in line with its metrical position as an anacrusis to the last two-bar unit. The constant shifting between major- and minor-mode associations centred

Example 22. II/164–9

on B and G♯ in Bars II/161–3 is underpinned by the fact that the tonic triads of both B major and G♯ minor lie within the scale of E major.

At the beginning of the second phrase (Example 22), the cadential point of departure (II/164) is again marked by a clear harmonic reference. This dominant seventh on F♯ is associated with the C⁷ chord in the following bar through an octatonic collection to which, with the exception of the last beat of II/164, the linear motion in these two bars is also aligned. The F minor association of the C⁷ chord comes into play in II/166, before an octatonic allegiance is again deducible at II/168 through successive dominant-quality chords on C♯, B♭ and G. Although during II/169 the gamut shifts from pure octatonic to pure whole-tone, the final sonority maintains a relation with the former model by virtue of its dominant-quality voicing on B♭.

As the phrase proceeds from II/170, the allegiances to extended tonal

Example 22 (cont.)

collections change at an approximately half-bar rate, and this pulse – giving momentum to the music as the soloist is joined by the orchestral strings – is all the more perceptible for the close alignment of the sonorities in II/170–3 with a number of familiar harmonic schemata. The last two bars of the phrase (II/176–7) settle on an octatonic/whole-tone complex around an E^7 chord, similar to that which opened the variation at II/158. In this way, the cadential articulation clearly indicated by the tempo markings is once again supported by a secure harmonic reference.

The harmonic correspondence between II/158 and II/177 might appear to suggest that the reading of the whole variation should be unified in some way, but this is difficult to accomplish conscientiously. The perceived centricity around G# and B in II/161–3, for example, might be conceived in terms of a quasi-Schenkerian arpeggiation of the E major triad, but it is better thought of as arising from the articulation of the chorale melody in the bass. This melody has a stylistic familiarity which lends it a stronger cohesive force than any quasi-Schenkerian interpretation could claim,[29] as well as conforming to Schoenberg's view of the crucial role of the theme in suspended tonality.

Ironically, an ideological conviction that analytical readings should be structurally unified might equally suggest that tonal alignments of the sort identified here are so brief, and so rapidly shifting, that to set them out explicitly is to overemphasise them at the expense of the 'unifying' serial context. The sketches do indeed confirm that the music of the variation was composed serially, but only the derivation of the opening horn chords (P_{10}) and the *Klagegesang* (see Example 19, p. 82) is clear, and the general imperceptibility of the series denies it any central interpretative function. In contrast to the specious certainty of a serial analysis, the fragmentation evident in the account given here reflects a coherence which arises through recognition rather than structuration. And since the interpretative strategies underlying this comprehension have emerged from an examination of wider stylistic issues, it is to that context that any remaining difficulties must return.

Form and programme as context

Despite all the foregoing discussion of tonal orientation in the serial writing of certain passages, it is clear that in other parts of the concerto the alignment of the music with tonal schemata is far more difficult for the listener or analyst to accomplish. Some passages, such as the opening of Part II and the climax at II/125, plainly achieve their effect through the projection of dissonant sonorities as forceful musical gestures, so that the assimilation of these into a tonalistic reading, were it even possible, would misrepresent their dramatic impact. While the music's tendency to move into and out of tonal focus is particularly evident at the turning-point between Parts IIa and IIb – and underlined by a stylistic allusion that is apparent even to a listener who does not specifically know either the chorale or its words – the situation elsewhere is more fluid. Returning once again to I/200–7 (Example 13, pp. 72–3), it will be seen that the flute and clarinet arabesques are not always in scalar alignment with the harmonic schemata on which attention was focused in earlier discussion. Clearly, the notes in question are serial remnants resulting from the extraction of harmonies whose prominence in the texture is maintained by the rhythmic and instrumental articulation. At the same time, however, these notes are far from inaudible: a delicate balance is involved whereby the tonal reading remains at once self-evident, besieged, and yet still viable.

A similar principle operates also on the larger scale, where the concerto's constant stream of tonalistic configurations both invites and fails to secure an integrated tonal reading of the work. As in the first Chorale Variation, the beginnings and ends of phrases are frequently supported by clear harmonic references, and these could readily be taken out of context and placed in sequence to give a second-level harmonic summary of the work; the tonal orientations listed earlier (pp. 65–6) could then be extracted at a third level. These interrelated analyses would not constitute an organic tonal reading, however, but instead would confirm at several levels, large and small, the situation identified by Schoenberg in respect of his Second String Quartet. Just as the large-scale G minor centricity in Part I of the concerto is merely fitful, so the harmonies which are heard at cadences cannot be said to represent the entirety of the phrases concerned. In each case, the reductive process is not one of assimilation but of selection:[30] the items chosen for re-presentation at the next level are merely taken for themselves, in recognition of their identity with external musical data. This iconic function of the harmonic references at cadence-points is in line with the tendency, noted constantly in chapter 4, for the harmony to remain static while the cadences are articulated by other, textural means. In all these respects, as Berg put it in 1930, the 'yearning for familiar concords' is stronger than 'the holy commandments of tonality'.[31]

This process of interpretation is nevertheless akin to an organic tonal reading, in that it cannot be unidirectional, proceeding only from the musical surface. As the layout of this chapter indicates, it works also from the largest level inwards, with the most prominent references cueing the recognition of further elements through alignment with tonal schemata; these in turn invite further interpretation along the same lines and ultimately encourage the tonalistic perception of the detailed musical fabric. But the continuity of musical perception thus achieved is an illusion – just as the continual correlation of the musical gestures with the well-known dramatic programme of the work gives the false impression of a continuous musical narrative. The music is not organically, self-referentially coherent, but 'makes sense' because at every point *something* in it is always recognisable through an active cognitive framework. The music of II/1 and II/125, for example, cannot participate directly in the tonalistic reading, which must be literally suspended at these points, but these passages are accepted into the listener's overall participation in the work as 'dramatic gestures' which may be correlated with the programme. On the other hand, the reprise of the Allegro at II/96, which has no clear programmatic function, is brought by way of compensation into the orbit of the work's extended tonality through the textural separation of elements of C♭ major and F major within a twelve-note complex. The recapitulatory aspect of II/96 binds these two deeply contrasting passages together – demonstrating that formal archetypes not only throw specific musical features into relief (Jarman's 'tonal centres') but can also promote connections between elements which might otherwise fail to cohere.

Almost by definition, this way of reading coherence into the Violin Concerto through constant reference to external musical archetypes has been unable to assert the kind of self-referential unity which Schenkerian tonal analysis might aim to show. But in fact this kind of unity is a myth even in 'common-practice' tonal music of the eighteenth and early nineteenth centuries, not least because it is this common practice, rather than any individual piece itself, which provides the models of harmonic progression, linear motion and so forth, in terms of which such 'unity' is charted. Only piece-specific materials such as themes and motives can participate in genuine self-referentiality; and while such writing seemed in the years before the 1914 war to be some kind of ideal in the minds of progressive composers of Schoenberg's generation, it was generally abandoned in the genuine modernism of the 1920s. The introspective, almost self-communing works written by Skryabin in his last years supplied a restricted musical language whose vogue was inevitably as brief as its subsequent eclipse was to be total. Schoenberg, on the other hand, formalised the self-referential principle in the technique of serial composition, which allowed for greater integration of this kind than had been seen in music hitherto. While Webern followed this path, pursuing the classicism inherent in Schoenberg's formalistic approach, Berg tackled the larger problems which had been exposed. The tension between internal and external reference which is so clearly focused in his last work has a profoundly historical dimension which is merely hinted at by its accommodation of pre-existing melodies.

6

Reception and critical evaluation

The early reception of the concerto was, inevitably, conditioned by the exaggerated ideological discord of its era. The Vienna premiere (see pp. 44–5) was a case in point: Klemperer's high-profile commitment – matching that of Kleiber in his Berlin premiere of the *Lulu Suite* two years previously – was directly opposed by the criticism which appeared in the Nazi-orientated popular press. But the Germanic nations were not alone in associating the music of the Schoenberg school with a subversive ideology. In a newspaper review of Webern's performance of the concerto in London, the prominent critic Ernest Newman wrote not of atonality, but of 'atonalism':

> No one, of course, would venture to lay it down, a priori, that atonalism could not express, say, the plain man's feelings about such things as love or death: but we were at least entitled to ask for a practical demonstration that a modern atonal Romeo could sing something to his Juliet which the rest of us would wish to overhear, or a mourning nation follow atonally a hero to his tomb. This evidence was not forthcoming; yet, until it was, there was no hope of atonalism sweeping the world.[1]

Newman's talk of 'atonalism sweeping the world' is symptomatic of the way he chose to redraw the musical ideologies of his day in the image of the larger political conflict of the 1930s, with its tendency towards polarisation and imperialism. With ironical use of the political metaphor 'true-blue', an adjective normally applied to persons unhesitatingly loyal to the British Conservative party, he went on to raise an issue which was to become a recurring point of debate in discussions of Berg's music, and this work in particular – that is, whether the 'tonal' and 'atonal' elements were in conflict or in balance:

> Here, under the stress of profound grief over the death of someone he had loved, he quotes a melody from a Bach cantata, giving it us first of all in what we may call normal harmony, then harmonised atonally. But surely atonalism of the true-blue type is one thing and tonalism quite another, and never the twain shall meet? An atonal composer surely ought to think all of a piece atonally; his melody, for instance, ought to be

organically one with his harmony, as tonal melody is organically one with tonal harmony. To take an existing tonal melody – the product of a certain way of thinking in music – and then give it atonal harmonies – the product of a completely different way of musical thinking, and directed towards a completely different end – is to fall between two stools.[2]

The political characterisation was completed by casting Schoenberg in the role of a Stalin or a Hitler, and Berg as the heroic dissenter, doomed to a struggle within himself. With this supposed inner conflict already silenced by Berg's death, Newman was free to make a saccharine prediction of 'what might have been', in metaphorical reflection of the political hopes of himself and his British readers:

To what extent was his adoption of atonalism due merely to the influence of Schönberg, and to what extent did he continue, out of pure loyalty, to profess his master's faith before the world while in his heart of hearts dissenting from it, or at any rate from a good deal of it? . . . [I suspect] that Berg was all along a composer divided against himself, pulled in one direction by that strange influence which Schönberg seems to have exercised upon all the young people who came into personal contact with him, and in another direction by his own inborn bias towards the main German tradition. If we draw a line through the later portions of 'Wozzeck', the Lyrical Suite, 'Lulu' and the violin concerto, it is not very difficult to surmise what would have been the outcome of that conflict within him had he lived another ten or twenty years.[3]

This review was characteristic of the early stages of a modern work's reception, in that it moved quickly to general issues; the Violin Concerto was used as a pretext for a discussion of Berg's style, perceived as a whole and set within the larger context of the Schoenberg school. Newman focused nevertheless on some major questions raised specifically by the concerto; less knowledgeable critics, even twenty years later, would continue to use the work as a springboard for the discussion of serialism or even atonality in general, and it was later still that the concerto was sufficiently familiar for individual performances to be routinely evaluated in terms of their own qualities.

Seen historically, the points chosen for discussion in critical writings on the concerto, and the contexts set for such debate, have traversed a complex network. The tendency of early writers to seize the opportunity to discuss the Schoenberg school in the broad context of twentieth-century music was exacerbated by the place in the repertoire which the concerto gained during the 1950s. Then, through a kind of tokenism, Berg's music came to stand in the popular imagination for the music of the three Viennese; the Violin Concerto, together with *Wozzeck*, became furthermore an index of his own output as a whole.[4] Thus, while Berg was liable to be a scapegoat for anti-modernist critics, his music, and the concerto in particular, was at the same time used as a lever for the habilitation of twelve-note music. The conservatism of Berg's late style, noted immediately by Newman and by most later writers also, could conveniently be overlooked by the first group; critics of the latter persuasion, for their part, were inclined to gloss over the question of possible linguistic inconsistency between the serial passages and the tonal *objets trouvés* in the concerto. In contrast to these two groups, writers whose social function was less didactic found Berg's music correspondingly less central to their aesthetic concerns. Different though their anatomies of musical modernism were, both Adorno (1949) and Donald Mitchell (1963) set up Schoenberg and Stravinsky as opposing keynote figures by means of which to objectify the dialectical oppositions through which their arguments could be pursued.[5]

As suggested above, early mentions of the Violin Concerto tended to be set within discussions of Berg's music, or the music of the Schoenberg school in general. A notable example is found in Aaron Copland's *Our New Music* (1941):

As far as actual creative achievement goes, the composer most generally acclaimed of all the Schoenberg school has been his pupil, Alban Berg . . . Berg managed to normalize the Schoenberg idiom by relating it more frankly to its Tristanesque origins. By comparison with his master's tortuous personality, Berg seems warm and sweetly human. His operas *Wozzeck* and *Lulu*, his *Violin Concerto*, and the *Lyric Suite* for string quartet are among the finest creations in the modern repertoire.[6]

Like Ernest Newman, but for different reasons, Copland also predicted that atonalism would not 'sweep the world'. Essentially, his view was that the music of the Schoenberg school was elitist – which, for Copland, meant that it could not fulfil the social function of 'our new music'. Cunningly expressing his faint praise in the language of genuine appreciation, he struck directly at the modernist credentials of the Schoenberg school by damningly asserting that this was music of the past, not the future:

Certain pages of these works are of a magical inspiration – sensuously lyrical, violently dramatic and profoundly erotic by turns. This does not change the essential truth that Berg's music belongs to the German past . . . [It] is music that, despite the modern means employed, sends us back to an emotional experience the essence of which we have thoroughly lived through. In that sense, it must reluctantly be admitted, it is music without a future . . . [Being] the expression of a highly refined and subtle musical culture, it has very little for a naïve but expanding musical culture such as is characteristic today of the United States . . . [and] is likely to be of interest principally to specialists and connoisseurs rather than to the generality of music lovers.[7]

A similar assessment of the work's content was expressed in 1949 by Virgil Thomson, reviewing a performance of the concerto by Szigeti in New York:

German expressionism at its most intense and visceral is the work's esthetic. The twelve-tone row technique is the method beneath its coherence. Pure genius is the source of its strength . . . Expressive chiefly of basic pleasure–pain and tension–relief patterns . . . its few cerebral references (to a Viennese waltz in the first movement and a harmonized Bach chorale in the last) stand out like broken memories in a delirium.[8]

Thomson's appreciation of the work, like Copland's, was evidently somewhat generalised, and indeed uncommitted – he wrote that it was 'removed from [his] personal sensibilities' and that he had never found his emotions transported by it. But the post-war respect now due to the Schoenberg school led him also to assert, in contrast to Copland, that the concerto would have a secure place in the future repertoire; in the absence of any deeper understanding of the work, however, he could merely argue that this would be on account of its 'perfection'.

Post-war orthodoxies

The idea that the concerto was, if not perfect, then at least beyond serious criticism – casting the work in the image of the 'angel' it had commemorated – had come into general circulation in the context of the pro-Schoenbergian propaganda published by, among others, René Leibowitz.[9] According to this new orthodoxy, whose Darwinian basis caused it to be widely accepted, Schoenberg's innovations were the inevitable results of an evolutionary process: they answered the 'crisis' which tonality faced at the end of its harmonic and polyphonic evolution from Bach and Mozart to Weber, Schubert and the Romantics and thence to Wagner. Just as modality had inevitably given way to tonality, so tonality had inevitably given way three centuries later. After 'the suspension of the tonal system' from c. 1908, the introduction of the serial method allowed 'the coherent development of a musical thought': here was the new system which historical necessity demanded. This ideology undoubtedly owed much to the writings of Schoenberg himself. Berg, too, had presaged this view in 1930, when he paralleled the supposedly pivotal historical positions of Bach and Schoenberg in an article revealingly entitled 'Credo'.[10] Leibowitz's portrayal of the Violin Concerto nevertheless expanded considerably upon the 'official' view of the work put forward by Berg's confidant and spokesman Willi Reich in 1937.[11] Whereas Reich had been content to point out the triads and the whole-tone

scale within the row, and to mention the coincidence of its last four notes with
the opening of the chorale melody – making no claims about the integration
of the Bach harmonisation or the recreation of a tonal language – Leibowitz
both saw the chorale genre as a rightful part of Berg's immediate heritage and
claimed explicitly that the two kinds of writing, while separately identifiable,
were integrated under the twelve-note system:

The harmonization and the variation of the chorale are among the most strictly
traditional elements of Schoenberg's teaching. There is no doubt the young Berg,
during his apprenticeship, had to devote many arduous hours to the study of these
forms . . . So it is not surprising that Berg, having attained the height of mastery, again
approaches, traditionally as well as radically, those forms which link the Schoenbergian
universe with the previously evolved world of music.

This link is also found in the restoration of certain tonal functions within the total
resources of chromaticism . . . [Because of the triadic structure of the row] it comes
about that certain treatments of [it] permit the elaboration of many 'classical' tonal
functions (such as the tonic-dominant type of progression) [here Leibowitz quotes bars
I/11–15]. On the other hand it is evident that combinations very different from those
of tonality result with equal frequency, but, thanks to the twelve-tone row technique,
form a coherent part of the total harmonic structure . . .[12]

Being modern and at the same time the natural outcome of tradition, serial
technique, it seemed, could from its position at the summit of musical
achievement to date encompass all it surveyed.

But to the new generation of serialists emerging into post-war Europe from
Messiaen's analysis class in Paris, Berg's tonalist conservatism was anachro-
nistic: the serial and tonal 'languages' were – as Newman from his very
different perspective had maintained – incompatible. Pierre Boulez was the
polemicist for this group, and in a commentary on various works of Berg
performed in Paris in 1948, he singled out the Violin Concerto for especial
criticism in this regard:

Berg seems to me to have committed a serious error . . . at the end of his Violin Concerto
in writing his variations on the Bach chorale 'Es ist genug!' I am well aware that certain
cunning theorists will hurl these arguments at me: (i) that the chorale is perfectly
integrated into Berg's score through the tritone shared by the last four notes of the
series and the four opening notes of the chorale; (ii) that the twelve-note system allows
this, being so rich in possibilities that it encompasses both tonality and atonality. This
is all ratiocination and verbiage! In the exposition of the chorale, where Berg's serial
harmonisation alternates with the tonal harmonisation by Bach, there is an unacceptable break in continuity on account of the hybridisation between the tonal system in
which the melody fully resides and the twelve-note system. I do not reject the principle

of a serial harmonisation of a Bach chorale because of the so-called true harmony which is found within a melody. But it is necessary to choose one or the other of these solutions, rather than cast them together; the materials are not of the same nature, the structure cannot but be without justification and without stability. This is cruelly apparent to the ear. Besides, I believe that the twelve-note language has more pressing tasks than to tame a Bach chorale.[13]

Over the next two decades, other specialist European writers on serial music also inclined towards this viewpoint, albeit less stylishly than Boulez, and generally by omission rather than by direct criticism. It is of course hardly surprising that Berg's music did not feature in the pages of *Die Reihe*, the journal devoted to the new ideas of Boulez, Stockhausen and their colleagues in the 1950s and 1960s, for whom Webern had shown 'The Path to the New Music'. But even those writers principally concerned with the earlier wave of serial composition played down Berg's position in the Viennese triumvirate. Josef Rufer's 'Composition with Twelve Tones' (1952) was concerned almost entirely with the works of Schoenberg, and, in the same year, Hanns Jelinek's 'Introduction to Twelve-Tone Composition' dealt almost exclusively with works by Schoenberg, Webern, and – Jelinek! In the 1960s both Herbert Eimert and Reginald Smith Brindle were also more concerned with Schoenberg and Webern than with Berg.[14] Webern evidently received coverage in recognition of his importance for the composers of the day, and Schoenberg, as the inventor of the row, could hardly have been excluded. But, apart from a certain amount of commentary on the all-interval series of the *Lyric Suite*, and the anecdotal mention of the Violin Concerto's triadic row as a point of curiosity, Berg's serial writing seems to have been irrelevant to these writers – music of the past, as Copland had predicted.

Towards a popular appreciation

Berg's exclusion from the concerns of the new modernists did not cause him to be hailed by anti-modernist critics, however, as is illustrated by an astonishing piece of writing by Martin Cooper (1954), which revived the political metaphor seen in the 1930s – now in terms of the Cold War:

Atonality stands in the same relation to previous music as Communism stands to the political tradition of Western Europe, and it was a perfectly healthy instinct that dubbed the music of Schoenberg and his pupils *Kulturbolschewitsch* ['cultural Bolshevist']. But since all revolutionaries must have been born and grown up . . . in the tradition against which they eventually revolt, it is inevitable that they perpetuate their own personal reactions and experiences under the old régime in the 'new world' they create . . . Schönberg and his disciples, growing up in the last days of the Austrian Empire, imbibed the atmosphere of shiftlessness and hopelessness inseparable from social, political and artistic bankruptcy. The new music sprang, therefore, from [this] world of over-heated emotionalism, morbid and hysterical . . . Inevitably it bore the mark of its origins deeply ingrained and the combination of this pathological nature with the intense Jewish analytical intellectuality of Schönberg has been the distinguishing mark of atonality hitherto.[15]

Clearly, this rather confused outburst was directed at all sorts of music besides Berg's, and certainly not at the Violin Concerto in particular. It was against this kind of phobia that Mosco Carner (1952) directed a fine article on the concerto, sympathetic in sensibility and notably shrewd in argument.[16] Carner approached his readers cautiously, constructing his argument in the context of their presumed prejudices, and continually pre-empting criticism. Thus he apologised in advance for the necessarily technical language of parts of his discussion; he shadow-boxed against anti-modernist and anti-intellectual stances, giving ground over the admittedly 'artificial and arbitrary' nature of the series; he played on Schoenberg's bogey-man image, suggesting that the 'humane' Berg had 'succeeded' by 'bending Schönberg's system to his own artistic will'. Schoenberg's chromaticism was excessive, admitted Carner reassuringly, but Berg had 'brought about a kind of *rapprochement* with tonal music'. Both the serial method and the concerto itself were cleverly explained in terms presumed central to the musical and cultural world of his readers: the series was 'something between a scale, a key and a basic theme'; the Bach chorale was a natural expression of Protestant religious feelings;[17] the role of the soloist linked Berg's work with Elgar's Cello Concerto and its use of waltz and ländler rhythms followed the 'time-honoured tradition' of the classics.

When, two decades later, Carner came to write a monograph on Berg, all this special pleading was either dropped or heavily adjusted.[18] But this was perhaps more a reflection of the different cultural environment of the mid-1970s than of an assumption that the readers of a book specifically on Berg would be sympathetic, for Hans Redlich's fine study of the composer's music (1957) had also included a preface less populist than Carner's article, but cautious nonetheless in its expression of the Leibowitzian orthodoxy.[19] The revised edition of Willi Reich's book (1963), on the other hand, presumed Berg's classic status, and in 1979 Douglas Jarman was able to compare the security of Berg's reputation with the restricted availability of his scores.[20]

With regard to the concerto, Redlich, Jarman and George Perle expressed differing views on the question of musical language raised by the quotation of the folk song and the chorale. Redlich suggested that the work 'grows out of the thematic cells of certain quotations from existing melodies, which thus become structural determinants for the whole work'; among the three principal thematic elements (the series, the folk song and the chorale melody) he, like Boulez, identified a linguistic opposition – not between the series and the other two, however, but between the folk song and the chorale, which, though 'diametrically opposed', were 'fused' in the transitional passage between them towards the end of the work (bars II/198–203).[21] This was a view which gave priority to motivic-thematic unity in the Schoenbergian manner: harmony, tonality and other elements of the music could be expected to serve this larger order without necessarily showing unity themselves. Perle actually developed Boulez's position further, applying it to the general musical language of the concerto rather than the treatment of quoted material. In his view, the work offered no general model for harmonic organisation in serial music, which could not 'depend upon a borrowed harmonic language, based upon premises that have no general meaning in the twelve-tone system'.[22] At the same time, this formulation did not deny that the music of the concerto itself was linguistically integrated. Perle's assertion that the serial technique of the concerto was subject to constraints external to its systematic integrity was consistent with his long-held view that the thematic and motivic relations pursued in the musical texture of *Lulu* depended more on specific configurations of pitches than on abstract serial relations. Jarman's more direct analysis of the question hinged on ideas of confrontation and reconciliation: the introduction of the chorale melody was typical of a Bergian tendency to bring together apparently conflicting elements, but, since the serial music of the concerto in general was 'tonally orientated', Jarman argued, 'the conflict between the tonal and twelve-note material is not as great as it might have been.' In Jarman's view, Berg's serial harmonisation of 'Es ist genug' did indeed effect a reconciliation between two types of material; without echoing Leibowitz's view that the serial method had somehow encompassed the language of the chorale, he pointed out that the manner in which Berg had handled the chorale melody was 'indicative of the intellectual fascination which the mechanics of twelve-note composition exerted upon him'.[23]

Conflict or resolution?

The finest individual essay to appear on the Violin Concerto during this time came from Adorno (1963).[24] Written in the form of an address to performers, it is largely taken up with a chronological discussion of the work, illuminated by well-considered observations on detailed questions of interpretation and articulation. Adorno's writing has the clear-headed sophistication to be expected of a great philosopher, while his period of musical study as a pupil of Berg gave him a unique double qualification. But his proximity to the Schoenberg circle did not prevent him from expressing a strong antagonism to certain works, nor did his rigorous intellectualism prevent him from changing his mind. His views of the concerto are an illustration of this: whereas in 1949 he had argued, with reference to the programmatic turning-point of Part II, that '[dissonance] as a symbol of disaster and consonance as a symbol of reconciliation are neo-romantic relics',[25] he now perceived that the later Berg had striven for 'a congruence of method and material'.[26] And while he had formerly identified a weakness in Berg's inability to renounce anything at his disposal, 'whereas the power of all new music lies precisely in renunciation',[27] he later accepted the co-existence, even the 'coalescence', of tonal and serial aspects, observing that '[the] double sense of the material, as both twelve-note and at the same time quasi-tonal . . . informs the whole structure'.[28] At the same time, he developed a central idea from his earlier discussion of the work, that the music attempts the impossible: not only a 'premature reconciliation' – which, while lending an 'intense inner beauty' to Berg's last works, was inferior to the antagonisms left exposed in Schoenberg's music – but also a 'morbidly mournful sacrifice of the future to the past',[29] a 'musical death-wish' whose mechanism he explained thus:

The Bergian artwork seeks to reconcile two plainly contradictory things: to dissolve itself and yet to remain its own master. Only through the utmost exertion of his ability to shape his material can he realise this idea of the amorphous, the genuinely in-formal, without his music becoming feebly swallowed up by it – without the artwork that objectifies chaos sinking into chaos itself. No less strong than the desire towards nothingness is that towards articulation; Berg's ubiquitous urge to fashion the shapeless in its own image [*das Gestaltlose als Gestaltloses gestalten*]. In a piece which sets up so few oppositions within its differential continuum as the Violin Concerto, such continuity could be saved from monotony only because Berg at the same time so fashioned it that the supreme plasticity of each composed moment is implicated in the seamless interconnectedness of each and every moment. Everything is transitory, and yet everything must immediately show itself for what it is. The entire abundant tradition of music, from Viennese classicism to Schoenberg, finds itself in company with a compositional spirit that not only leaves no style untouched, as if it were self-possessed and isolated, but fundamentally opposes each one, treats all as nothing.[30]

This argument sets the tone for a discussion in which the performer is exhorted to characterise each moment in such a way that it paradoxically merges into the continuity of the whole.

Another eminent commentator whose view of the concerto changed over the years was Boulez, who by the post-structuralist 1970s felt closer to Berg than to Webern. In contrast to the latter, whose music he now found lacking in depth, Boulez perceived in Berg the richness of ambiguity, as he explained in terms not far short of Adorno's habitual paradoxes:

... what I find in Berg ... is a sense of continuous development with an enormous degree of ambiguity – what I call a 'romanesque' or novel-like development – that is, we no longer have a simple architectural development with points of symmetry (always an easy standpoint to adopt) but on the contrary we have much more intricate forms which virtually never cease to develop and imply no return to earlier material ... [By] combining forms that were very much established and, as a rule, clear and preconceived, with an acute sense of development ... he charged them with so much ambiguity that they take on a totally different meaning and virtually cease to exist. This evolution accomplished by Berg can only be seen as part of a continual quest for maximum effectiveness in these forms, which is no sooner found than there is only one desire – to progressively break up and destroy them, or to so overload them with emotional and formal additions that they collapse under all the extra weight. History as it is made by great composers is not a history of conservation but of destruction – even while cherishing what is destroyed.[31]

At the same time, Boulez was still unable to accept the 'co-existence between different grammars and styles' within the Violin Concerto:

In [this] case . . . it is a *dramatic gesture*. I do not think it is a very profound gesture – indeed I find rather that it expresses anxiety; perhaps even rejection of the norms of contemporary behaviour. There is a sort of nostalgia for a bygone world that you find again much later in works of quite recent days . . . To my way of thinking, if one is to preserve certain aspects of the past and to integrate them into our present-day thought, it must be done in the most abstract terms.[32]

If, as Boulez suggests, the treatment of the chorale in the concerto shows Berg merely cherishing the past, without in this instance simultaneously destroying it, then in Adorno's terms this might be seen as a lack of opposition to the style concerned – an unwillingness to treat it as nothing.

And so we return to the crucial turning-point, both musical and programmatic, in the Violin Concerto: the point where death itself is engaged in musical terms which seem, both paradoxically and inconsistently, to neglect for the moment the drive towards stylistic integration through liquidation. Yet Boulez's analysis of this as a 'dramatic gesture' demands further investigation: how can such drama come about – and what exactly is it? The unalloyed presentation of the Bach style sets up an antithesis which some, including Newman and Boulez, have rejected as an incongruity; others have seen, in the progress of the Adagio from this point towards its final cadence, a linguistic reconciliation symbolising acceptance in the face of death. The possibility of reconciliation, like Adorno's 'opposition', suggests antagonism rather than mere antithesis, but, as Thomas Clifton observed, writing in the late 1970s, it is only one of two possible outcomes:

Two . . . important aspects of the agonic [are] the stalemate and the reconciliation. The difference . . . is . . . that in the former, the antagonists remain in a contesting frame of mind, and they are still equals in strength. Furthermore, the events unfolding the play are such that it is impossible to determine whether one antagonist overcomes the other. On the other hand . . . reconciliation . . . is constitutive of every concerto I have ever heard – I think particularly of Berg's Violin Concerto . . .[33]

Clifton went on to discuss Stravinsky's *Agon* (1953–7), finding in this work the 'complex unity, breaking down either-or distinctions', which he saw as characteristic of reconciliation.[34] Composed astride Stravinsky's neoclassical and serial periods, *Agon*, like Schoenberg's Second String Quartet, is a work which, within itself, expresses the drama of stylistic change. Berg's concerto is different, in that it was written several years after the composer had reached the turning-point to which serialism had led him: more importantly, its stylistic *agon* is not purely Bergian, but instead suggests a broader conflict.

If, as Adorno argued, Berg's encounters with new stylistic possibilities led him not to cross the rubicons of atonality and serialism, but rather to compose music which, by perpetually breaking down stylistic distinctions, was in a constant state of reconciliation, then the encounter with Bach raised for once the possibility of stalemate. Arnold Whittall (1987) expressed the view that the rhetoric of the Adagio shows Berg emphasising linguistic conflict rather than reconciling it; that the first statement of the chorale is 'a powerful representation of the synthesis of connection and conflict' which is transformed through the Coda's resolute 'anti-Bachness' into a 'disturbing exploration of [the] opposing tendencies within the [series] itself'.[35] The suggestion is that perhaps in accordance with an autobiographical programme, Berg chose this moment to throw into question the entire basis of his art, by demonstrating that even the use of a series whose immanent tonalism was remarkably fulsome could not produce a synthesis. Instead, one might say, he showed how the chorale style lay on the other side of history, untouchable, beyond the grave.

Boulez's 'drama' operates on several levels, therefore, the first of which straightforwardly exploits the chorale as a *coup de théâtre*, consistent with the work's 'official' programme. Beyond this, the potential outcomes of an idealised conflict are explored in this most agonic of genres. The possibility of linguistic reconciliation is raised through the progress of the chorale – particularly in the Coda, where the ancient melody and texture are apparently united with serial harmony. But, at the same time, the music also suggests the ultimate impossibility of such reconciliation, as Whittall describes. If these readings seem contradictory, this might add a suitable element of infinite regression: a work which simultaneously, and indeed similarly, celebrates both reconciliation and confrontation might be said at the same time to have reconciled – and yet not reconciled – those two inseparable and eternal opposites.

Notes

1 Musical ideologies: style and genre in the 1930s

1 Schoenberg, 'National Music (2)', in *Style and Idea*, pp. 173–4.
2 Van den Toorn, *The Music of Igor Stravinsky*; Heinrich Schenker, *Das Meisterwerk in der Musik*, vol. 2 (Munich: Drei Masken Verlag, 1926), pp. 37–40.
3 Igor Stravinsky & Robert Craft, *Dialogues* (London: Faber, 1982), p. 47.
4 Vera Stravinsky & Robert Craft, *Stravinsky in Pictures and Documents* (New York: Simon & Schuster, 1978), p. 306.
5 I. Stravinsky & Craft, *Dialogues*, pp. 47–8.
6 V. Stravinsky & Craft, *Stravinsky in Pictures and Documents*, p. 348.
7 These original compositions should not be confused with the arrangements of works by Monn and Handel which Schoenberg made in 1932–3.
8 Igor Stravinsky & Robert Craft, *Expositions and Developments*, 2nd edn (London: Faber, 1981), p. 147.

2 Towards the Violin Concerto

1 This tally excludes the brief canon written for the 50th anniversary of the Frankfurt Opera House in 1930 (published in Reich, *Alban Berg* (1937), supplement, p. 16); it also omits the suite of five symphonic pieces compiled in 1934 from the music of *Lulu*.
2 Berg's constructive reaction to Schoenberg's criticism – which in any case was more specifically directed at the clarinet pieces – and the scandal which attended the first performance of selections from the *Altenberg Lieder* on 31 March 1913, has not prevented the ultimate appreciation of the musical qualities of these songs.
3 Letter of 9 July 1913, Berg to Schoenberg (Brand et al. (eds.), *The Berg–Schoenberg Correspondence*, p. 182).
4 Reich, *Alban Berg* (1937), p. 17.
5 Jarman, *Alban Berg: Wozzeck*, pp. 157, 159.
6 Jarman, *The Music of Alban Berg*, p. 12.
7 Redlich, *Alban Berg*, p. 63.
8 Igor Stravinsky & Robert Craft, *Conversations with Igor Stravinsky*, 2nd edn (London: Faber, 1979), p. 72.
9 Perle, *The Operas of Alban Berg*, vol. 1: *Wozzeck*, p. 17.
10 Adorno, *Alban Berg*, pp. 81–2 (my translation).
11 Perle, *The Operas of Alban Berg*, vol. 1: *Wozzeck*, pp. 12–13.
12 Igor Stravinsky & Robert Craft, *Memories and Commentaries*, 2nd edn (London: Faber, 1981), p. 110.
13 In his preface to the miniature score (Vienna: Universal Edition, 1927).

14 Jarman, *The Music of Alban Berg*, pp. 148–52.
15 Letter of 9 February 1925, Berg to Schoenberg (Brand et al. (eds.), *The Berg–Schoenberg Correspondence*, pp. 334–7); Brenda Dalen, '"Freundschaft, Liebe, und Welt": the secret programme of the Chamber Concerto', in Jarman (ed.), *The Berg Companion*, pp. 141–80.
16 Letter of 13 July 1926, Berg to Schoenberg (Brand et al. (eds.), *The Berg–Schoenberg Correspondence*, p. 351).
17 For further discussion of Berg's rhythmic techniques, see Jarman, *Alban Berg*, pp. 147–74, and 'Some Observations on Rhythm, Metre and Tempo in *Lulu*'.
18 Perle, *The Operas of Alban Berg*, vol. 2: *Lulu*, pp. 68–84.
19 For an English translation see Jarman, *Alban Berg: Wozzeck*, pp. 154–70.
20 Joseph Kerman, *Opera As Drama* (New York: Random House, 1956), pp. 225, 229, 232.
21 Jarman, *The Music of Alban Berg*, p. 4.
22 Letter of 13 July 1926, Berg to Schoenberg (Brand et al. (eds.), *The Berg–Schoenberg Correspondence*, pp. 349–50).
23 Perle, 'The Secret Program of the *Lyric Suite*'; Green, 'Berg's De Profundis: The Finale of the *Lyric Suite*'.
24 The cryptography of Berg's references to keys in his letter to Schoenberg is in fact yet more remarkable: as well as the major-key pairs C/F$\sharp$ and F/B (i.e. F–H: Hanna Fuchs), the notes concerned also lie within the scales of the corresponding minor keys – either A/E♭ or D/A♭. In his letter to Schoenberg, Berg specifically mentions the first of these minor-key pairs, whose tonic pitches are in German spelled as A and Es (pronounced 'S'), i.e. A–S, the initials of Schoenberg himself. There can be little doubt that this additional homage to his Master was fully intentional. By mentioning A–Es and F–H in the same breath, as it were, Berg perhaps risked the discovery of his love for Hanna. But, by reversing the order of her initials, he may have hoped to set up the smokescreen of an apparent allusion to the composer who had 'discovered' this all-interval series, his pupil Fritz Heinrich (F.H.) Klein, who had already used the series in his Variations for piano, Op. 14 (1924).
25 Letter of 10 January 1927, Berg to Schoenberg (Brand et al. (eds.), *The Berg–Schoenberg Correspondence*, p. 357). Details of other plays to which Berg gave consideration may be found in Carner, *Alban Berg*, 2nd edn, p. 71.
26 Adorno, *Alban Berg*, pp. 32–3.
27 Letter of 17 January 1928, Webern to Berg (Jarman, *The Music of Alban Berg*, pp. 10–11); letter of 3 [March] 1928, Schoenberg to Berg (Brand et al. (eds.), *The Berg–Schoenberg Correspondence*, p. 365).
28 Werfel, *And the Bridge is Love*, p. 174; the date of their meeting is given as 30 January in Reich, *Alban Berg* (1937), p.15.
29 Letter of 30 March 1928, Berg to Schoenberg (Brand et al. (eds.), *The Berg–Schoenberg Correspondence*, p. 366).
30 Letter of 26 April 1928, Berg to Schoenberg (Brand et al. (eds.), *The Berg–Schoenberg Correspondence*, p. 369).
31 A musical motive intended for Pippa was inscribed in the visitors' book of Dr Alfred Kalmus on 3 May 1928 (reproduced in Carner, *Alban Berg*, 2nd edn, p. 72); an early sketch for the Prologue to *Lulu*, later discarded, is dated 23 June 1928 (see Ertelt, '"Hereinspaziert . . ."'). Berg's use of the fateful '23' on this sketch may indicate that he regarded it as the outset of work on the opera itself.
32 Both the orchestral and piano versions of the songs were finished by 10 April 1928, together with the string orchestra arrangement of three movements from the *Lyric Suite* (letter of 10 April 1928, Berg to Schoenberg, in Brand et al. (eds.), *The Berg–Schoenberg Correspondence*, p. 369).
33 Berg's work on the reduction and other chores connected with the publication and premiere of the *Gurrelieder* occupied him on and off for two years from the spring of 1911; his guide to the work was published by Universal Edition in 1913 (see Select bibliography).

34 Perle, *The Operas of Alban Berg*, vol. 1: *Wozzeck*, p. 3.
35 Letter of 1 September 1928, Berg to Schoenberg (Brand et al. (eds.), *The Berg–Schoenberg Correspondence*, p.373).
36 Letters of 17 January 1929 [completed and posted in February] and 7 May 1929, Berg to Schoenberg (Brand et al. (eds.), *The Berg–Schoenberg Correspondence*, pp. 382, 387). The premiere of the Three Orchestral Pieces took place on 14 April 1930.
37 The full score of *Der Wein* was dated 23 August 1929, but since Berg habitually affixed his fateful number 23 to important letters, documents and manuscripts, this date is not necessarily precise. In a letter to Schoenberg dated 26 August, however, he reported the completion of the aria, saying also that he intended to return immediately to *Lulu* and to work on the opera 'at least until the end of September' (Brand et al. (eds.), *The Berg–Schoenberg Correspondence*, p. 388).
38 Letter of 20 September 1929, Berg to Webern, quoted in Hall, 'The Progress of a Method', p. 500.
39 See Hall, *ibid.*, pp. 512, 518n19. Hall reports that Berg's draft from this date reached 'ca. m. 520'; in the published score there is a double bar-line at bar 521, while one of the new series which Berg introduced in the next phase of the opera's composition appears at bar 523.
40 Charles Baudelaire, *Die Blumen des Bösen*, trans. S. George, (Berlin: Bondi, 1922).
41 Reich, *Alban Berg* (1965), pp. 79–80; see also Hall, 'The Progress of a Method', pp. 501–2.
42 The exception is the Painter, whose musical character was fully established before the decisive technical developments of Autumn 1929. For further details as communicated to him by Berg, see Reich, *Alban Berg* (1937), pp. 112–13; for an extension of Reich's method of description to other series and other characters, see Reiter, *Die Zwölftontechnik in Alban Bergs Oper LULU*.
43 Jarman, *The Music of Alban Berg*, pp. 96–101; see also Pople, 'Serial and Tonal Aspects of Pitch Structure in Act III of Berg's *Lulu*'.
44 Letter of 30 August 1929, Reich to Berg. This discussion is indebted to the account of Reich's letter given in Hall, 'The Progress of a Method', p. 501.
45 Jarman, *Alban Berg: Lulu*, pp. 68–75.
46 The musical prominence in the opera of the 'common areas' between its many series caused the Berg scholar George Perle to question the validity of Reich's account (see 'The Music of *Lulu*: A New Analysis' and *The Operas of Alban Berg*, vol. 2: *Lulu*, pp. 93–121). The documentary evidence supporting Reich's account is incontrovertible, however, and Perle's analysis must be regarded as a case of special pleading for the audible over the inaudible, when it is clear that Berg's conception comprised both dimensions.
47 Letter of 7 August 1930, Berg to Schoenberg (Brand et al. (eds.), *The Berg–Schoenberg Correspondence*, p. 405).
48 For details of the early productions of *Wozzeck*, see Jarman, *Alban Berg: Wozzeck*, pp. 69–80.
49 Letter of 6 August 1931, Berg to Schoenberg (Brand et al. (eds.), *The Berg–Schoenberg Correspondence*, p. 414).
50 Reich, Alban Berg (1937), pp. 118–19; Perle, *The Operas of Alban Berg*, vol. 2: *Lulu*, pp. 149–57.
51 Letter of 17 November 1931, Berg to Schoenberg (Brand et al. (eds.), *The Berg–Schoenberg Correspondence*, p. 424).
52 Letter of 13 December 1932, Berg to Schoenberg (Brand et al. (eds.), *The Berg–Schoenberg Correspondence*, p. 437).

3 Composition and performance history

1 Figures taken from Brand et al. (eds.), *The Berg–Schoenberg Correspondence*, pp. xxvii, 446n3, 449 (the last of these being a letter of 6 December 1933, Berg to Schoenberg).
2 Letter of 6 December 1933, Berg to Schoenberg (Brand et al. (eds.), *The Berg–Schoenberg Correspondence*, p. 450). Mrs Coolidge's own financial position had deteriorated by this time

as a result of the Wall Street crash, but she continued nevertheless to sponsor a gallery of leading modern composers.

3 Letter of 27 March 1934, Schoenberg to Berg (Brand et al. (eds.), *The Berg–Schoenberg Correspondence*, p. 451).

4 In a letter to Helene dated 9 March 1934, Berg wrote: '. . . now it looks as though I've found the right notes for both [Geschwitz's] closing stanzas' (Grun (ed. & trans.), *Alban Berg: Letters to his Wife*, p. 424); surprisingly, he seems not to have been able finally to report the completion of the opera to Webern until 6 May (Reich, *Alban Berg* (1965), pp. 92–3).

5 For further details of the chronology of Berg's work on *Lulu* during 1934 see Cerha, *Arbeitsbericht*, pp. 4–6.

6 A letter of 8 October 1935 to Helene indicates that, before the end of his life, Berg entertained the hope that *Lulu* might be produced in Prague (Grun (ed. & trans.), *Alban Berg: Letters to his Wife*, p. 429). The first production of the incomplete two-act version of the opera took place in Zurich in 1937.

7 Krasner was born in Cherkassky (now in USSR) in 1903, and was brought up in the USA from the age of five. Much of the information given here on his commissioning of Berg's concerto is collated from Krasner, 'The Origins of the Alban Berg *Violin Concerto*', pp. 107–17 and the account given in Carner, *Alban Berg*, 2nd edn, pp. 85–7, which derives from consultation with Krasner. Krasner's subsequent career also included the premiere of Schoenberg's Violin Concerto in 1940; he was concertmaster of the Minneapolis Symphony Orchestra from 1944 to 1949 and later taught at the University of Syracuse, NY.

8 Presumably this was the performance which took place on 24 November 1931.

9 Arrangements for this performance had been made by the end of January 1935 (Letter of 30 January 1935, Berg to Schoenberg, Brand et al. (eds.), *The Berg–Schoenberg Correspondence*, p. 463); it took place on 22 March.

10 Krasner, 'The Origins of the Alban Berg *Violin Concerto*', p. 110.

11 According to Reich, this was in February 1935 (*Alban Berg* (1937), p. 126), the date perhaps being the 23rd.

12 Krasner, 'The Origins of the Alban Berg *Violin Concerto*', p. 110.

13 Erich Alban Berg, *Der unverbesserliche Romantiker*, p. 114.

14 These Variations, which feature an obbligato solo violin throughout, comprise bars 83–230 of Act III of *Lulu*. For an analysis of the music, see Pople, 'Serial and Tonal Aspects of Pitch Structure in Act III of Berg's *Lulu*', pp. 45–9, 54–7.

15 It was probably coincidental, however, that Berg had recently renewed his working acquaintance with a violin concerto texture when arranging the Adagio of the Chamber Concerto for violin, piano and clarinet for a concert in honour of his fiftieth birthday, which fell on 9 February 1935.

16 Krasner, 'The Origins of the Alban Berg *Violin Concerto*', pp. 110–11.

17 Letter of 28 March, Berg to Krasner ('Zur Entstehung des Violinkonzertes von Alban Berg', p. 196). Mahler, too, used to compose at his country home on the Wörthersee.

18 Reich, *Alban Berg* (1965), p. 99.

19 Werfel, *And the Bridge is Love*, pp. 87, 128.

20 *Ibid.*, p. 210.

21 ÖNB Musiksammlung, F 21 Berg 85/I, fol. 1, 1v, 2, 2v.

22 *Ibid.*, F 21 Berg 85/II, fol. 10.

23 Letter of 28 August 1935, Berg to Schoenberg (Brand et al. (eds.), *The Berg–Schoenberg Correspondence*, p. 466). In view of this violinistic conception, it seems extraordinary that it was the transposition of the series beginning with D♭ to which Berg gave the Roman numeral 'I' in his row table.

24 ÖNB Musiksammlung, F 21 Berg 85/II, fol. 8.

25 *Ibid.*, F 21 Berg 432/XV (Tagebuch 1935), p. 161. The tabular presentation given here has been facilitated by the transcription of the sketch given in Floros, 'Die Skizzen zum

Violinkonzert von Alban Berg', p. 119.

26 Letter of 20 January 1936, Charley Berg to Frida Semler Seabury, quoted in Donald Harris, 'Berg and Miss Frida', p. 205.

27 ÖNB Musiksammlung, F 21 Berg 85/II, fol. 35*v*.

28 Reich, *Alban Berg* (1965), p. 101.

29 ÖNB Musiksammlung, F 21 Berg 85/I, fol. 6, reproduced in Floros, 'Die Skizzen zum *Violinkonzert* von Alban Berg', p. 124.

30 ÖNB Musiksammlung, F 21 Berg 85/I, fol. 8.

31 *Ibid.*, fol. 3.

32 Reich, *Alban Berg* (1965), p. 102.

33 *Ibid.*, pp. 178–9.

34 Jarman, 'Alban Berg, Wilhelm Fliess and the Secret Programme of the Violin Concerto', pp. 185–92.

35 Translation adapted from Knaus, 'Berg's Carinthian Folk Tune'.

36 The child, born on 4 December 1902, was acknowledged by her father and named Albine. Douglas Jarman has suggested (*Alban Berg: Wozzeck*, p. 67) that this episode in Berg's life is one of several elements linking the composer autobiographically with the protagonist of his first opera, whose companion, also named Marie, is the mother of his illegitimate child.

37 ÖNB Musiksammlung, F 21 Berg 85/II, fol. 21*v*.

38 Because Berg attempted to draft the insertion directly into the *Particell*, he inevitably made mistakes and so had to discard otherwise neat pages (ÖNB Musiksammlung, F 21 Berg 85/ II, fol. 22, 22*v*).

39 Krasner, 'The Origins of the Alban Berg *Violin Concerto*', pp. 107–8, 111.

40 *Ibid.*, p. 111.

41 Hence his belief that Berg did not decide to use 'Es ist genug' until June (Reich, *Alban Berg* (1965), p. 101).

42 Roth (ed.), *60 Choralgesänge von Johann Sebastian Bach*.

43 ÖNB Musiksammlung, F 21 Berg 85/II, fol. 34*v*, reproduced in Floros, 'Die Skizzen zum *Violinkonzert* von Alban Berg', p. 123.

44 A discarded sheet from the *Particell* of Part II carries the marking *à la marcia* at II/23 (ÖNB Musiksammlung, F 21 Berg 85/II, fol. 1); the marking was revised to *molto ritmico*.

45 ÖNB Musiksammlung, F 21 Berg 85/II, fol. 3, reproduced in Floros, 'Die Skizzen zum *Violinkonzert* von Alban Berg', p. 125.

46 Floros, 'Die Skizzen zum *Violinkonzert* von Alban Berg', p. 131.

47 ÖNB Musiksammlung, F 21 Berg 432/XV (Tagebuch 1935), p. 162, transcribed in Floros, 'Die Skizzen zum *Violinkonzert* von Alban Berg', p. 120.

48 ÖNB Musiksammlung, F 21 Berg 85/I, fol. 8.

49 *Ibid.*, F 21 Berg 85/II, fol. 21*v*.

50 Schoenberg, *Fundamentals of Musical Composition*, pp. 58, 153.

51 A facsimile of the *Particell* of II/4–5 appears in Lorkovic, 'Später Versuch einer Textkorrektur im Violinkonzert von Alban Berg', p. 612.

52 See Lorkovic, 'Berg's Violin Concerto: Discrepancies in the Published Score'; Conridge, 'A Wrong Note in Berg's Violin Concerto?'; Perle, *The Operas of Alban Berg*, vol. 2: *Lulu*, p. 245. Conridge's identification of an obvious error in Berg's transcription of the Bach chorale harmonisation (II/143), though scrupulously correct, is hilariously laboured, and he overlooks a similar error a bar earlier; Lorkovic identifies one crucial transcription error between the *Particell* and the full score (II/4–5), together with a number of other possible errors deduced by analysis of the serial structure – not always a reliable guide in this work – and supported by a study of the autograph *Particell* and full score, but not the continuity draft and sketches. Perle's suggested emendation to the evidently garbled solo part in bar II/95 is based on commonsense rather than a study of the manuscripts, and does not correspond with the continuity draft, which appears to have G/D♭ at the point where Perle suggests G/E♭. The

critical edition edited by Douglas Jarman – not yet in print at the time of writing – is likely to be definitive.

53 Letter of 16 July 1935, Berg to Krasner ('Zur Entstehung des Violinkonzertes von Alban Berg', p. 196). The date of 12 July given for the completion of the *Particell* in Redlich, *Alban Berg*, p. 269 is based on a letter of 15 July (NB) from Berg to Webern concerning the broadcast on 12 July of Webern's orchestration of the six-part Ricercar from Bach's *A Musical Offering*, in which Berg writes: '. . . I was so dog-tired after a working day of almost thirteen hours that I was unable to cope with music any more and went to bed. You see, I had that day [12 July] as good as finished the composition of the Violin Concerto, sitting from seven in the morning until nine in the evening almost uninterruptedly at my piano or writing-desk.' Although Redlich does not quote the earlier part of this letter, it would seem that Berg was excusing himself for having failed to hear the broadcast, and so perhaps allowed himself to exaggerate the importance of his day's work a little; in any case, he does not say that he literally finished the composition on that day, merely that it was 'as good as finished' [*soviel wie beendigt*]. The date of 23 July given by Reich (*Alban Berg* (1937), p. 17) can be discounted as merely yet another instance of the number 23 being used superstitiously in connection with an important occasion in Berg's life.

54 Letter of 16 July 1935, Berg to Krasner ('Zur Entstehung des Violinkonzertes von Alban Berg', pp. 196–97).

55 In a letter to Webern of 7 August, Berg wrote: 'In a week's time I hope to be able to write to you further. Just now I'm working furiously on my score so as to get it finished by mid-August, and so am leaving everything else to one side' (Redlich, *Alban Berg*, p. 269). During a weekend visit to the Waldhaus on 10 and 11 August, Willi Reich played through the work as a piano duet with the composer, who remarked that he was 'pleased by the unexpectedly rapid completion of the work', but in view of Berg's progress report to Webern this ought probably not to be taken to mean that the full score was literally complete by the 9th. If Berg wanted urgently to play through the work with Reich before sending the *Particell* of Part I to Krasner in Switzerland, he may have been happy to put the finishing touches to it afterwards. In his biography of the composer, Reich evidently assumed that this was done on the day of his departure (*Alban Berg* (1937), p. 17); but as Berg, in a letter of 14 August to Ruzena Herlinger's husband, wrote that he finished the concerto 'the day before yesterday' (Jarman, 'Two Unpublished Letters from Berg'), it seems most likely that the concerto was completed on 12 August 1935. Berg sent the remaining *Particell* material to Krasner the next day (letter of 13 August 1935, Berg to Krasner, 'Zur Entstehung des Violinkonzertes von Alban Berg', p. 197), and the score was sent to Universal Edition on the 14th, with a note asking for it to be engraved 'in C' – i.e. with the transposing instruments notated at concert pitch (letter of 14 August 1935, Berg to Hans Heinsheimer, extract quoted in Cerha, *Arbeitsbericht*, p. 31).

56 Letter of 13 September 1935, Berg to Krasner ('Zur Entstehung des Violinkonzertes von Alban Berg', p. 197). What is now the viola part at I/77–8 was originally to have been taken by the soloist above a fingered tremolo in single notes (B, D♯).

57 Helene Berg, interview (n.d.) with Erich Schenk, cited in Jarman, *The Music of Alban Berg*, p. 13n2.

58 Letter of 16 July 1935, Berg to Krasner ('Zur Entstehung des Violinkonzertes von Alban Berg', p. 196).

59 Kerner, 'Alban Bergs Ende', p. 112. Internal and circumstantial evidence suggests that this article was either written by, or published on behalf of, Willi Reich.

60 *Ibid.*, p. 113.

61 Krasner, 'The Origins of the Alban Berg *Violin Concerto*', p. 108.

62 Letter, dated 'mid-August 1935', Berg to Reich (Reich (ed.), *Alban Berg: Bildnis im Wort*, p. 77).

63 Letter of 26 August 1935, Berg to Reich (Reich (ed.), *Alban Berg: Bildnis im Wort*, p. 77).

64 Berg's decision was made between 26 and 28 August. See Moldenhauer, *Anton Webern*, pp.

448–9, and Berg's letter to Schoenberg of 28 August 1935 (Brand et al. (eds.), *The Berg–Schoenberg Correspondence*, p. 466). The Festival had been moved from Karlsbad for political reasons.

65 Kerner, 'Alban Berg's Ende', p. 112.

66 Letter of 12 October 1935, Berg to Helene Berg (Grun (ed. & trans.), *Alban Berg: Letters to his Wife*, pp. 433–4).

67 *Ibid.*

68 Reich, *Alban Berg* (1937), p. 17.

69 Kerner, 'Alban Berg's Ende', p. 112. Members of the composer's family later expressed the view that it was additional treatment given by this doctor which caused the fatal spread of sepsis through Berg's system (Erich Alban Berg, *Der unverbesserliche Romantiker*, pp. 116–17; also Helene Berg, reported in Vondenhoff, '"Es war eine Freundschaft vom ersten Augenblick an"', p. 607).

70 Letter of 4 November 1935, Berg to Reich (Reich (ed.), *Alban Berg: Bildnis im Wort*, p. 77).

71 Reich, *Alban Berg* (1937), p. 17.

72 Letter of 30 November 1935, Berg to Schoenberg (Brand et al. (eds.), *The Berg–Schoenberg Correspondence*, p. 469).

73 Joan Allen Smith, 'Berg's Character Remembered', pp. 28–9.

74 Reich, *Alban Berg* (1937), pp. 17–18. As Krasner's accompanist, Frau Dr Kurzmann might well have been asked to make the piano arrangement even had Erwin Stein, who had prepared the vocal score of *Der Wein* and was to do the same for *Lulu*, not himself been incapacitated after suffering a burst appendix in the summer.

75 Kerner, 'Alban Bergs Ende', p. 112. According to Hans Moldenhauer, Helene Berg later penned an account of Berg's final illness which was 'a bitter denunciation of the medical profession' (Moldenhauer, *Anton Webern*, p. 678n7). This account has not yet been published.

76 Kerner, 'Alban Bergs Ende', p. 112. Berg's pupil Leonhardt Märker was among the donors (Jarman, '"Man hat auch nur Fleisch und Blut": Towards a Berg Biography').

77 Reich, *Alban Berg* (1937), p. 18.

78 Letter of 20 January 1936, Charley Berg to Frida Semler Seabury, quoted in Donald Harris, 'Berg and Miss Frida', p. 205.

79 Reich, *Alban Berg* (1937), p. 18.

80 Kerner, 'Alban Bergs Ende', p. 112.

81 Moldenhauer, *Anton Webern*, p. 453.

82 Krasner, 'The Origins of the Alban Berg *Violin Concerto*', pp. 112–13.

83 Moldenhauer, *Anton Webern*, p. 455.

84 The account in this paragraph derives from information given in Moldenhauer, *Anton Webern*, pp. 455–6.

85 This was the first evening concert of the Festival. The programme was: Edmund von Borck, *Prelude and Fugue*; Roberto Gerhard, *Ariel* (ballet suite); Ernst Krenek, *Three Fragments from 'Karl V'*; Berg, Violin Concerto; Berg, *Three Fragments from 'Wozzeck'* (Slonimsky, *Music Since 1900*, 4th edn, pp. 624–5).

86 Letter of 26 April 1936, Benjamin Britten to Grace Williams, in Lewis Foreman (ed.), *From Parry to Britten: British Music in Letters 1900–1945* (London: Batsford, 1987).

87 Krasner, 'The Origins of the Alban Berg *Violin Concerto*', p. 113.

88 Krasner, 'The Violin Concerto in Vienna', p. 3.

89 Krasner, 'The Origins of the Alban Berg *Violin Concerto*', p. 114.

90 The information given here on these early performances in Europe and America is taken in general from Krasner, 'The Origins of the Alban Berg *Violin Concerto*', pp. 114–15. The London recording is attested to by Moldenhauer in *Anton Webern*, p. 679n12.

91 Walker, 'An Alban Berg Discography', p. 10.

92 Vondenhoff, '"Es war eine Freundschaft vom ersten Augenblick an"', p. 610n11.

93 See Boulez, 'Incidences actuelles de Berg' for a discussion arising from these performances.

94 Walker, 'An Alban Berg Discography', p. 10.
95 David Cox, *The Henry Wood Proms* (London: British Broadcasting Corporation, 1980), pp. 175, 179.
96 Rostal & Keller, 'Berg's Violin Concerto: a Revision'; Lorkovic, 'Berg's Violin Concerto: Discrepancies in the Published Score', p. 271.

4 Form, materials and programme

1 Letter of 28 August 1935, Berg to Schoenberg, reproduced in facsimile in Rufer, 'Dokumente einer Freundschaft', pp. 42–3; for an English translation see Brand et al. (eds.), *The Berg–Schoenberg Correspondence*, p. 466.
2 Perle draws attention to the slow–fast–fast–slow sequence of tempos in the concerto (*The Operas of Alban Berg*, vol. 2: *Lulu*, p. 243), at the same time noting that the contrast between the first two of these is minimal (the quaver pulse actually remains constant) while the third and fourth movements are more distinctly different in this respect.
3 Perle (*The Operas of Alban Berg*, vol. 2: *Lulu*, p. 244) reads a sonata-form exposition (only) here, but this is difficult to reconcile with the details of his analysis. Redlich (*Alban Berg*, p. 275) reads movement IIa (!) in sonata form, but this statement is unsupported and would appear to contradict Reich's assertion that a sonata-form design was considered by the composer for this movement and then abandoned (*Alban Berg* (1937), p. 128).
4 Schoenberg's classic discussions of the principle of 'developing variation' are to be found in 'Criteria for the Evaluation of Music' and 'Brahms the Progressive', both in *Style and Idea*, pp. 124–36, 398–441.
5 cf. Reich, *Alban Berg* (1937), p. 131.
6 Antony Beaumont (*Busoni the Composer* (London: Faber, 1985), p. 143) has drawn attention to the similarity between I/1 of the concerto and a passage in Busoni's *Berceuse élégiaque* (1909).
7 This phenomenon effectively deconstructs the very idea of 'cadence'; the terminology will be retained, however, for want of an alternative.
8 Reich, *Alban Berg* (1937), p. 129.
9 Although the *Hauptrhythmus* is established at this point, it is not marked as such (with the symbol RH) until II/119.
10 See Jarman, *The Music of Alban Berg*, pp. 139–40 for a serial analysis of II/35–8.
11 Rostal & Keller, 'Berg's Violin Concerto: a Revision'; Lorkovic, 'Berg's Violin Concerto: Discrepancies in the Published Score', p. 271.
12 Berg's *Particell* has 'darnieden' (to rhyme with 'Frieden'), rather than the full score's 'darnieder' (Lorkovic, 'Berg's Violin Concerto: Discrepancies in the Published Score', p. 269).
13 Reich, *Alban Berg* (1937), pp. 122–3.
14 As Douglass M. Green has pointed out ('Cantus Firmus Techniques in the Concertos and Operas of Alban Berg', p. 63), this canonic imitation at the fifth follows the pattern of II/135–6 (violas, solo violin) and II/158–9 (cellos, harp).
15 The value attached to this passage by Hans Redlich is discussed on pp. 97–8.
16 See Perle, 'The Secret Program of the *Lyric Suite*'.
17 Jarman, 'Alban Berg, Wilhelm Fliess and the Secret Programme of the Violin Concerto'; see also Berg's letter to Schoenberg, 20 June 1915 (Brand et al. (eds.), *The Berg–Schoenberg Correspondence*, pp. 248–9).
18 It has been suggested that this number might simply represent the number of letters in her name (Stadlen, 'Berg's Cryptography', p. 176), a theory which discounts the fact that her full surname was Fuchs-Robettin, giving eighteen letters in all. The name Helene Berg also contains ten letters, and the full name of Alban Maria Johannes Berg contains twenty-two (not twenty-three): it cannot be said, therefore, that there is conclusive evidence to support guesswork along these lines.

19 Reich's programme avoids the specific when it mentions 'the lovely image of the girl' in connection with the second appearance of the folk tune (*Alban Berg* (1937), p.128).

20 *Ibid.*, p. 131.

21 In German-speaking countries, E♭ is written 'Es', and so is pronounced identically with the letter S.

22 Berg seems not to have been concerned to check the accuracy of more complex calculations, however: in his letter to Schoenberg of 20 June 1915 (see note 17) he quotes Fliess as calculating the number of days in a year as $(28^2 + 28 - 23)/4 = 365$, which is utterly incorrect.

23 Jarman, 'Alban Berg, Wilhelm Fliess and the Secret Programme of the Violin Concerto', p. 185–7. Jarman's table consistently shows '23' in connection with sections of 22 bars – presumably because the first bar of the *next* section is the 23rd from the beginning of the original section – although his use of '10', '20' and '28' is arithmetically correct. Andras Pernye has pointed out in this regard that Manon died on 22nd of the month ('Alban Berg und die Zahlen', p. 156).

24 Despite this double bar-line, the appearance of '175' in the marginal calculations quoted by Jarman, together with the sketch evidence discussed on p. 34 and the change of time-signature at I/176, tends to support the formal analysis made in this chapter.

25 The numerology of the Chamber Concerto is based on 3 and its multiples – representing the trinity of the Schoenberg school.

26 Jarman, 'Alban Berg, Wilhelm Fliess and the Secret Programme of the Violin Concerto', p. 190.

27 This is most clear in the *ossia* version of the solo part, but the 'extra' notes in the preferred version, E and G, turn Berg's initials into his whole name – as paraphrased in the Chamber Concerto. Jarman's proposition is based straightforwardly on the HF which appears in the beat before the chorale phrase. Both anticipations of the chorale in the Allegro (II/43, II/68) outline the tritone FH or HF.

28 Jarman, 'Alban Berg, Wilhelm Fliess and the Secret Programme of the Violin Concerto', p. 192.

29 Reich, *Alban Berg* (1937), p. 126.

30 The extraordinary similarity of the concerto's design to the Andante–Ländler–Allegro–Adagio sequence of movements in Mahler's ninth symphony might be taken as an indication that Berg – like Mahler in that work – had thought to confront and yet evade fate.

31 Perle, *The Operas of Alban Berg*, vol. 2: *Lulu*, p. 59.

5 Harmony, tonality and the series

1 Schoenberg, 'My Evolution', in *Style and Idea*, p. 86.

2 Adapted from Jarman, *The Music of Alban Berg*, p. 103.

3 James M. Baker, 'Schenkerian Analysis and Post-Tonal Music', in D. Beach (ed.), *Aspects of Schenkerian Theory* (New Haven: Yale University Press, 1983), p. 186.

4 Allen Forte, *The Structure of Atonal Music* (New Haven: Yale University Press, 1973). For an introductory discussion of analytical methods, including Schenkerian and Fortean approaches, see Jonathan Dunsby & Arnold Whittall, *Music Analysis in Theory and Practice* (London: Faber, 1988).

5 See, for example, Schmalfeldt, *Berg's Wozzeck*; Tethys Carpenter, 'The Musical Language of *Elektra*', in Derrick Puffett (ed.), *Richard Strauss: Elektra* (Cambridge University Press, 1989), pp. 74–106.

6 This relationship naturally only holds between the numbers of two set-classes which together might comprise twelve elements (e.g. 4–x and 8–x, or 3–y and 9–y).

7 Schoenberg, *Structural Functions of Harmony*, pp. 19–21.

8 *Ibid.*, pp. 1–3; Dahlhaus, *Between Romanticism and Modernism*, pp. 64–71.

9 Dahlhaus, *Between Romanticism and Modernism*, pp. 68–9.
10 Schoenberg, *Theory of Harmony*, pp. 383–4.
11 *Ibid.*, p. 384.
12 Schoenberg, *Structural Functions of Harmony*, p. 165.
13 *Ibid.*, p. 165.
14 Schoenberg, *Theory of Harmony*, p. 384.
15 Berg, 'Was ist atonal?'.
16 Berg, 'Warum ist Schönbergs Musik so schwer verständlich?'.
17 Schoenberg, *Structural Functions of Harmony*, p. 164.
18 Schoenberg, *Theory of Harmony*, pp. 383–4.
19 Notations such as [0,3,6,10] are used here to indicate the intervallic constitution of the chord-type in question. Such chords are described in close position, with 0 referring to the root: in this example, the other notes lie 3, 6 and 10 semitones above it (e.g. C, E♭, G♭, B♭).
20 Although the octatonic scale appears fleetingly in both *Tristan* and *Parsifal*, and can be heard in the fifth of Berg's *Altenberg Lieder*, it is more prominent in the Russian repertoire and has been most fully explored in Van den Toorn, *The Music of Igor Stravinsky*. But it also underlies Schoenberg's analysis, in the *Harmonielehre*, of the fourfold ambiguity by which the diminished seventh chord can be interpreted as the upper four notes of any of four dominant minor ninth chords each a minor third apart (*Theory of Harmony*, p. 194); the [0,4,6,10] sonority is also octatonic, and can function as a dominant in any of four diatonic contexts, major and minor, whose scalar pitch-class collections lie at a minor third's distance (e.g. F major, F minor, B major, B minor). The same octatonic scale contains a complementary sonority of the same type – [1,3,7,9], i.e. [0,4,6,10] transposed by a minor third – which is associated with the same diatonic collections – though now understood as (e.g.) A♭ major, G♯ minor, D♭ major and C♯ minor. And, just as any tritone-related pair of these diatonic collections will include all twelve pitch-classes, so do the whole-tone sets associated with the two complementary [0,4,6,10] sonorities (see Anthony Pople, *Skryabin and Stravinsky 1908–1914: Studies in Theory and Analysis* (New York: Garland, 1989), especially chapter 4).
21 Schoenberg, *Theory of Harmony*, p. 384.
22 Compare Jarman's analytical approach to *Wozzeck* in *The Music of Alban Berg*, pp. 46–71.
23 The alignment of the first four notes of the chorale melody with the ascending whole-tone scale at the end of the prime form of the series is well-known. The opening phrase of Bach's harmonisation, as quoted in the concerto (II/142–3) may in fact be aligned with the series at P_{10}, though there is no reason to assume that Berg was aware of this. There is no clear relationship between the Carinthian tune and the series.
24 The G♮ in the second trumpet part at the end of I/140 is arguably a misprint for the G♯ which would conform to the series.
25 Reich, *Alban Berg* (1937), pp. 112–13; Perle, *The Operas of Alban Berg*, vol. 2: *Lulu*, pp. 85–6.
26 The D♯ on the second quaver of I/82, together with its two grace notes, is a semitone higher than the series predicts.
27 The melodic characteristics of the *Klagegesang* (beginning at II/164) are discussed in Green, 'Cantus Firmus Techniques', pp. 62–7.
28 See, for example, the serial analysis of II/35–8 in Jarman, *The Music of Alban Berg*, pp. 139–40.
29 This is not to deny the possible saliency of a bass arpeggiation where no such foreground stylistic allusion is to be heard. See Pople, 'Serial and Tonal Aspects of Pitch Structure in Act III of Berg's *Lulu*', pp. 48, 57; Ayrey, 'Tonality and the Series (Berg)'.
30 This distinction is explored in William E. Benjamin, 'Models of Underlying Tonal Structure: How Can They Be Abstract, and How Should They Be Abstract', *Music Theory Spectrum*, 4 (1982), pp. 28–50.
31 Berg, 'Was ist atonal?', trans. Norton, p. 1315.

6 Reception and critical evaluation

1 Newman, 'Alban Berg's Violin Concerto', quoted in Reich, 'An Ernest Newman', p. 23.
2 *Ibid.*, p. 24.
3 *Ibid.*, pp. 23, 26.
4 As an informal pointer to this phenomenon, it is interesting to note that, of the ten examples by Berg quoted in Walter Piston's classic book on orchestration in 1955, eight were taken from the Violin Concerto. Apart from an example of artificial harmonics for the viola quoted from Schoenberg's partially serial *Serenade*, Op. 24, no twelve-note work by the other members of the Schoenberg school was mentioned.
5 Adorno, *Philosophy of Modern Music*; Donald Mitchell, *The Language of Modern Music* (London: Faber, 1963).
6 Copland, *Our New Music*, pp. 55–6.
7 *Ibid.*, pp. 56–7.
8 Thomson, 'Gloomy Masterpiece'.
9 Leibowitz, *Schoenberg and His School*.
10 Berg, 'Credo', repr. in Reich, *Alban Berg* (1937), p. 161.
11 Reich, *Alban Berg* (1937), pp. 128–33.
12 Leibowitz, *Schoenberg and His School*, pp. 165–6.
13 Boulez, 'Incidences actuelles de Berg', pp. 239–40 (my translation).
14 Josef Rufer, *Die Komposition mit zwölf Tönen* (Berlin: Max Hesses, 1952); Hanns Jelinek, *Anleitung zur Zwölftonkomposition* (Vienna: Universal Edition, 1952); Herbert Eimert, *Grundlagen der musikalischen Reihentechnik* (Vienna: Universal Edition, 1964); Reginald Smith Brindle, *Serial Composition* (London: Oxford University Press, 1966).
15 Cooper, 'Alban Berg', in Bacharach (ed.), *The Music Masters*, vol. 1, pp. 40–1.
16 Carner, 'Alban Berg (1885–1935)', in Hill (ed.), *The Concerto*, pp. 362–79.
17 Berg was in fact brought up as a Catholic.
18 Carner, *Alban Berg*.
19 Redlich, *Alban Berg*.
20 Reich, *Alban Berg: Leben und Werk* (Zurich: Atlantis, 1963); Jarman, *The Music of Alban Berg*.
21 Redlich, *Alban Berg*, pp. 270–2.
22 George Perle, *Serial Composition and Atonality: An Introduction to the Music of Schoenberg, Berg and Webern*, 4th edn (Berkeley: University of California Press, 1977), p. 91; first edn 1962.
23 Jarman, *The Music of Alban Berg*, p. 143.
24 Adorno, 'Alban Berg: Violinkonzert'.
25 Adorno, *Philosophy of Modern Music*, p. 108.
26 Adorno, 'Alban Berg: Violinkonzert', p. 187.
27 Adorno, *Philosophy of Modern Music*, p. 109.
28 Adorno, 'Alban Berg: Violinkonzert', p. 187.
29 Adorno, *Philosophy of Modern Music*, p. 109.
30 Adorno, 'Alban Berg: Violinkonzert', pp. 188, 189–90.
31 Boulez, *Conversations with Célestin Deliège*, pp. 17–18, 21.
32 *Ibid.*, p. 155.
33 Clifton, *Music as Heard*, p. 247.
34 *Ibid.*, p. 250.
35 Whittall, 'The Theorist's Sense of History', pp. 11–12.

Select bibliography

Adorno, Theodor W. *Philosophy of Modern Music*, trans. Anne G. Mitchell & Wesley V. Bloomster (London: Sheed & Ward, 1973); first publ. 1949 (in German)

'Alban Berg: Violinkonzert', in *Der getreue Korrepetitor: Lehrschriften zur musikalischen Praxis* (Frankfurt: Fischer, 1963), pp. 187–216

Alban Berg: Der Meister des kleinsten Übergangs (Vienna: Elisabeth Lafite, 1968)

Ayrey, Craig. 'Tonality and the Series (Berg)', in Jonathan Dunsby (ed.), *Models of Music Analysis* (Oxford: Blackwell, forthcoming)

Berg, Alban. *A. Schoenberg, Gurrelieder: Führer* (Vienna: Universal Edition, [1913])

'Warum ist Schönbergs Musik so schwer verständlich?', *Musikblätter des Anbruch*, 6 (1924); trans. as 'Why is Schönberg's Music so Difficult to Understand?', in W. Reich, *Alban Berg* (1965), pp. 189–204

'Credo', *Die Musik*, 24 (1930); repr. in W. Reich, *Alban Berg* (1937), p. 161

'Was ist atonal?' [radio interview with Julius Bistron], Wiener Rundfunk, 23 April 1930; partial transcript in *23*, 26/27 (8 June 1936), pp. 1–11; trans. M.D. Herter Norton as 'What is Atonality?', in N. Slonimsky, *Music Since 1900*, 4th edn, pp. 1311–15

Berg, Erich Alban. *Der unverbesserliche Romantiker: Alban Berg 1885–1935* (Vienna: Österreichische Bundesverlag, 1985)

Boulez, Pierre. 'Incidences actuelles de Berg (à propos de la Quinzaine de Musique autrichienne à Paris)', in *Relevés d'apprenti* (Paris: Seuil, 1966), pp. 235–40; first publ. (in French) in *Polyphonie*, ii (1948)

Conversations with Célestin Deliège (London: Eulenburg, 1976); from interviews conducted (in French) in 1972–4

Brand, Juliane, Christopher Hailey & Donald Harris (eds.). *The Berg–Schoenberg Correspondence* (Houndmills: Macmillan, 1987)

Carner, Mosco. *Alban Berg: The Man and the Work*, 2nd edn (London: Duckworth, 1983)

'Alban Berg (1885–1935)', in Ralph Hill (ed.), *The Concerto* (London: Penguin Books, 1952), pp. 362–79

Cerha, Friedrich. *Arbeitsbericht zur Herstellung des 3. Akts der Oper LULU von Alban Berg* (Vienna: Universal Edition, 1979)

Clifton, Thomas. *Music as Heard: A Study in Applied Phenomenology* (New Haven: Yale University Press, 1983), p. 247

Conridge, Graham. 'A Wrong Note in Berg's Violin Concerto?', *The Musical Times*, 130 (1989), pp. 205–7

Cooper, Martin. 'Alban Berg', in A.L. Bacharach (ed.), *The Music Masters*, vol. 1: *The Twentieth Century*, 2nd edn (Harmondsworth: Penguin Books, 1957), pp. 35–41

Copland, Aaron. *Our New Music: Leading Composers in Europe and America* (New York: McGraw-Hill, 1941)

Dahlhaus, Carl. *Between Romanticism and Modernism: Four Studies in the Music of the Later Nineteenth Century*, trans. Mary Whittall (Berkeley: University of California Press, 1980)

Dalen, Brenda. "'Freundschaft, Liebe, und Welt": the secret programme of the Chamber Concerto', in Douglas Jarman (ed.), *The Berg Companion*, pp. 141–80

Ertelt, Thomas F. "'Hereinspaziert . . .": Ein früher Entwurf des Prologs zu Alban Bergs "Lulu"', *Österreichische Musik Zeitschrift*, 41 (1986), pp. 15–25

Floros, Constantin. 'Die Skizzen zum *Violinkonzert* von Alban Berg', *Alban Berg Studien*, 2 (Vienna: Universal Edition, 1981), pp. 118–35

Green, Douglass M. 'Berg's De Profundis: The Finale of the *Lyric Suite*', *The International Alban Berg Society Newsletter*, 5 (1977), pp. 13–23

'Cantus Firmus Techniques in the Concertos and Operas of Alban Berg', *Alban Berg Studien*, 2 (Vienna: Universal Edition, 1981), pp. 56–68

Grun, Bernard (ed. & trans.). *Alban Berg: Letters to his Wife* (London: Faber, 1971)

Hall, Patricia. 'The Progress of a Method: Berg's Tone Rows for *Lulu*', *The Musical Quarterly*, 71 (1985), pp. 500–19

Harris, Donald. 'Berg and Miss Frida: Further Recollections of his Friendship with an American College Girl', *Alban Berg Studien*, 2 (Vienna: Universal Edition, 1981), pp. 198–208

Jarman, Douglas. 'Two Unpublished Letters from Berg', *The Musical Times*, 113 (1972), pp. 351–2

The Music of Alban Berg (London: Faber, 1979)

'Some Observations on Rhythm, Metre and Tempo in *Lulu*', *Alban Berg Studien*, 2 (Vienna: Universal Edition, 1981), pp. 20–30

'Alban Berg, Wilhelm Fliess and the Secret Programme of the Violin Concerto', in Jarman (ed.), *The Berg Companion*, pp. 181–94

Alban Berg: Wozzeck (Cambridge University Press, 1989)

Alban Berg: Lulu (Cambridge University Press, 1991)

'"Man hat auch nur Fleisch und Blut": Towards a Berg Biography', in David Gable & Robert P. Morgan (eds.), *Alban Berg: Historical and Analytical Perspectives* (Oxford University Press, forthcoming)

(ed.) *The Berg Companion* (Houndmills: Macmillan, 1989)

Kerner, Dieter. 'Alban Bergs Ende', *Melos*, 29 (1962), pp. 112–13

Knaus, Herwig. 'Berg's Carinthian Folk Tune', trans. Mosco Carner, *The Musical Times*, 117 (1976), p. 487

Krasner, Louis. 'The Origins of the Alban Berg *Violin Concerto*', *Alban Berg Studien*, 2 (Vienna: Universal Edition, 1981), pp. 107–17

'The Violin Concerto in Vienna', *The International Alban Berg Society Newsletter*, 12 (1982), pp. 3–4

Leibowitz, René. *Schoenberg and His School*, trans. Dika Newlin (New York: Philosophical Library, 1949); first publ. 1947 (in French)

Lorkovic, Radovan. 'Berg's Violin Concerto: Discrepancies in the Published Score', *The Musical Times*, 130 (1989), pp. 268–71

'Später Versuch einer Textkorrektur im Violinkonzert von Alban Berg', *Österreichische Musik Zeitschrift*, 44 (1989), pp. 611–19

Moldenhauer, Hans. *Anton Webern: A Chronicle of his Life and Work* (London: Gollancz, 1978)

Newman, Ernest. 'Alban Berg's Violin Concerto – Tonality and Atonality', *The Sunday Times*, 10 May 1936, quoted in Willi Reich, 'An Ernest Newman', *23*, 28/30 (1936), pp. 20–8

Perle, George. 'The Music of *Lulu*: A New Analysis', *Journal of the American Musicological Association*, 12 (1959), pp. 185–200

'The Secret Program of the *Lyric Suite*', *The International Alban Berg Society Newsletter*, 5 (1977), pp. 4–12

The Operas of Alban Berg, vol. 1: *Wozzeck* (Berkeley: University of California Press, 1980)

The Operas of Alban Berg, vol. 2: *Lulu* (Berkeley: University of California Press, 1985)

Pernye, Andras. 'Alban Berg und die Zahlen', *Studia Musicologica*, 9 (1967), pp. 141–61

Pople, Anthony. 'Serial and Tonal Aspects of Pitch Structure in Act III of Berg's *Lulu*', *Soundings*, 10 (1983), pp. 36–57

Redlich, Hans F. *Alban Berg: Versuch einer Würdigung* (Vienna: Universal Edition, 1957)

Reich, Willi. *Alban Berg: Mit Bergs eigenen Schriften und Beiträgen von Theodor Wiesengrund-Adorno und Ernst Krenek* (Vienna: Reichner, 1937)

The Life and Work of Alban Berg, trans. Cornelius Cardew (London: Thames and Hudson, 1965); first publ. 1963 (in German)

(ed.) *Alban Berg: Bildnis im Wort* (Zurich: Die Arche, 1959)

Reiter, Manfred. *Die Zwölftontechnik in Alban Bergs Oper LULU* (Regensburg: Bosse, 1973)

Rostal, Max & Hans Keller. 'Berg's Violin Concerto: a Revision', *The Musical Times*, 95 (1954), pp. 87–8

Roth, Herman (ed.). *60 Choralgesänge von Johann Sebastian Bach* (Munich: Drei Masken Verlag, 1920)

Rufer, Josef. 'Dokumente einer Freundschaft', *Melos*, 22 (1955), pp. 42–6

Schmalfeldt, Janet. *Berg's Wozzeck: Harmonic Language and Dramatic Design* (New Haven: Yale University Press, 1983)

Schoenberg, Arnold. *Fundamentals of Musical Composition*, ed. Gerald Strang (London: Faber, 1967); written 1937–48

Style and Idea, ed. Leonard Stein, with translations by Leo Black (London: Faber, 1975)

Theory of Harmony, trans. Roy E. Carter (London: Faber, 1978); first publ. 1911 (as *Harmonielehre*)

Structural Functions of Harmony, rev. edn, ed. Leonard Stein (London: Faber, 1983)

Slonimsky, Nicolas. *Music Since 1900*, 4th edn (London: Cassell, 1972)

Smith, Joan Allen. 'Berg's Character Remembered', in Douglas Jarman (ed.), *The Berg Companion*, pp. 13–32.

Stadlen, Peter. 'Berg's Cryptography', *Alban Berg Studien*, 2 (Vienna: Universal Edition, 1981), pp. 171–80

Stein, Erwin. [preface to Alban Berg, *Lyrische Suite*, miniature score] (Vienna: Universal Edition, 1927)

Thomson, Virgil. 'Gloomy Masterpiece', in *A Virgil Thomson Reader* (Boston: Houghton Mifflin, 1981), pp. 330–1; first publ. in the *New York Herald Tribune*, 16 December 1949

Van den Toorn, Pieter C. *The Music of Igor Stravinsky* (New Haven: Yale University Press, 1983)

Vondenhoff, Eleonore. '"Es war eine Freundschaft vom ersten Augenblick an"' [interview with Andreas Maul], *Österreichische Musik Zeitschrift*, 44 (1989), pp. 601–10

Walker, Arthur D. 'An Alban Berg Discography', *The International Alban Berg Society Newsletter*, 3 (1975), pp. 8–10

Werfel, Alma Mahler. *And the Bridge is Love* [trans. E.B. Ashton] (London: Hutchinson, 1959)

Whittall, Arnold. 'The Theorist's Sense of History: Concepts of Contemporaneity in Composition and Analysis', *Journal of the Royal Musical Association*, 112 (1987), pp. 1–20

'Zur Entstehung des Violinkonzertes von Alban Berg' [letters from Berg to Louis Krasner], *Musikblätter des Anbruch*, 18 (1936), pp. 196–7

Index

Adorno, Theodore W., 12, 16, 19, 93, 98–9, 100, 101
Ahle, Johann Rudolf, 58

Bach, David Josef, 27
Bach, Johann Sebastian, 2, 30, 56, 94; B–A–C–H motto, 17; *O Ewigkeit, du Donnerwort* (BWV 60), 36, 58
Baker, James, 66
Bartók, Béla, 1, 17, 18; Violin Concerto No. 2 (Sz 112), 5; Concerto for Orchestra (Sz 116), 8
Baudelaire, Charles, 19; *Les Fleurs du mal*, 21
Beethoven, Ludwig van, 2, 27; Violin Concerto in D, Op. 61, 35; Symphony No. 3 in E♭ ('Eroica'), Op. 55, 51; Symphony No. 7 in A, Op. 92, 46
Berg, Alban,
life: affair with Marie Scheuchl (1902), 34, 48, 61, 64; as disciple of Schoenberg, 6, 10, 11, 69–70, 92, 93, 97; financial and material circumstances in 1930s, 23–4, 25–6; illness and death, 37, 41–3, 63
music: elements of style, 6–7, 9, 11, 12–13, 16, 19–20, 99–100; use of textbook forms, 16, 23; use of symmetrical formal structures, 17–18, 23, 53; rhythmic techniques, 14–16; serial techniques, 13–14, 15–17, 22–3; tonal elements in serial works, 18, 20, 21; ciphers and numerology, 17, 18–19, 21, 61–64; posthumous composition plans, 10, 42
writings, 71, 94
Violin Concerto, 1, 3, 7, 9, 12, 20; commission, 5, 7, 26–7; dedication, 28, 94; preliminary work, 27–8; process of composition, 28–32, 34–40; process of

orchestration, 30, 40–41; preparation of piano score, 43; premiere, 43–4; performances to 1950, 44–46, 90–4, 95; recordings, 45–6; reception and critical evaluation, 7, 8, 60, 91–102; state of manuscript sources, 39–40; 'official' programme, 32–3, 37, 47–9, 60–1, 63, 89–90, 91, 100–1; 'secret' programme, 33–4, 37, 47–8, 60–4, 100–1; relationship between soloist and orchestra, 8, 50–60; formal structure, 30–1, 34–7, 47–60; serial technique, 22, 29, 31, 37–40, 50, 55, 56–7, 58, 59, 60, 66, 67–9, 75, 76–83, 88, 94–6, 97, 98, 101; tonality, 29, 31, 35–6, 50, 52, 53, 54, 57, 58–60, 65–6, 69–80, 81, 83–90, 95–6, 97; Carinthian folk song quoted, 13, 30, 33–4, 37, 48, 54, 59, 61, 63, 93, 94, 97–8; chorale setting ('Es ist genug'), 14, 30–1, 33, 34, 35–7, 41, 43, 48, 56, 57–60, 62, 63, 82, 88, 91, 93, 94, 95–6, 97, 98, 100–2; *Hauptrhythmus*, 14–16, 36, 55, 56, 57, 62; *Klagegesang*, 33, 59, 60, 81–2, 88
other works: *Altenberg Lieder*, Op. 4, 9–10, 11, 14; Chamber Concerto, 11, 13, 14, 16–17, 18, 46, 47, 61; *Der Wein*, 7, 9, 13, 15, 17–18, 20–1, 22, 25, 27, 40, 44, 47, 78; Four Pieces for clarinet and piano, Op. 5, 9–10, 11; *Lulu*, 9, 10, 11, 12, 13, 14, 15, 16 19, 20, 21, 22–4, 25, 26, 27, 29, 30, 31, 40–1, 42, 47, 48, 58, 63, 77, 80, 81 ,92, 93, 98; *Lulu Suite*, 10, 25–6, 27, 43, 91; *Lulu Symphony* (plan), 10; *Lyric Suite*, 9, 10, 13, 14, 15–16, 17–19, 21, 22, 26, 36, 46, 47–8, 61–2, 63, 77, 92, 93, 96; Piano Sonata, Op. 1, 9, 10–11, 26; *Seven Early Songs*, 9, 19–20; 'Schliesse mir die Augen beide' (1925 setting), 13, 18;

Index

Index

Nazi party (Germany), 25, 44, 91
Newman, Ernest, 91–2, 93, 95, 100

Österreichische Nationalbibliothek, 28
Ozawa, Seiji, 46

Paganini, Nicolò, 7
Pau Casals Orchestra (Barcelona), 44
Perle, George, 9, 11–12, 16, 20, 80, 97, 98
Perlman, Itzhak, 46
Poulenc, Francis, *Concert Champêtre* (harpsichord and orchestra), 3; Concerto in D minor (two pianos and orchestra), 3
Prokofiev, Sergey, 1; Violin Concerto No. 2 in G minor, Op. 63, 5
Puccini, Giacomo, 16

Rakhmaninov, Sergey, 1, 4, 5, 8; Piano Concerto No. 4 in G minor, Op. 40, 4, 5; *Rhapsody on a Theme of Paganini*, Op. 43, 4, 5; Symphonic Dances, Op. 45, 4; Symphony No. 3 in A minor, Op. 44, 4
Ravel, Maurice, Piano Concerto for the left hand, 3; Piano Concerto in G, 3
Redlich, Hans, 11, 97–8
Reich, Willi, 11, 22, 23, 28, 31, 32, 34, 35, 36, 42, 53–4, 58, 59, 60, 61, 80, 94–5, 97
Reihe, Die, 96
Rodzinski, Artur, 45
Rosé, Arnold, 45
Rossi, Mario, 45
Rufer, Josef, 96

Schenker, Heinrich, 2; theory of tonal structure, 66, 69, 87–8, 89, 90
Scherchen, Hermann, 44
Scheuchl, Albine, 34
Scheuchl, Marie ('Mizzi'), 34, 61
Schoenberg, Arnold, 1–2, 5, 6, 7, 10, 11, 12, 14, 15, 16, 17, 18, 19, 20, 24, 25, 29, 43, 47, 65, 66, 68, 69, 76, 88, 89, 90, 92, 93, 94, 95, 96, 97, 99
works: *Das Buch der hängenden Gärten*, Op. 15, 65; Chamber Symphony No. 1, Op. 9, 2, 10, 20; Chamber Symphony No. 2, Op. 38, 2; *Erwartung*, Op. 17, 6, 16; Five Orchestral Pieces, Op. 16, 6, 11; *Gurrelieder*, 20, 70, 79; *Pelleas und Melisande*, Op. 5, 20; Piano Concerto, Op. 42, 5; Serenade, Op. 24, 6; String

Quartet No. 1 in D minor, Op. 7, 2, 11, 71; String Quartet No. 2, Op. 10, 2, 11, 65, 70, 89, 101; Suite, Op. 29, 6; Suite in G (string orchestra), 5; Symphony (unfinished sketch, 1937), 5; Theme and Variations, Op. 43a, 5; Three Piano Pieces, Op. 11, 65; Two Songs, Op. 14, 65; Variations for Orchestra, Op. 31, 6; Variations on a Recitative, Op. 40, 2; Violin Concerto, Op. 36, 5; Wind Quintet, Op. 26, 6
writings: 2, 38–9, 65, 66, 70, 73, 94; *Harmonielehre*, 20, 69–70, 71–2, 76
'Schoenberg school' (S., Webern, Berg), 5, 7, 12, 14, 17, 18, 25, 26, 27, 91, 92, 93, 94, 96–7, 99
Schubert, Franz, 71, 94; 'Unfinished' Symphony in B minor (D. 759), 11
Seabury, Frida Semler, 30
Skryabin, Alexander, 90
Smith Brindle, Reginald, 96
Solti, Georg, 46
Stalin, Joseph, 92
Stein, Erwin, 14
Stern, Isaac, 46
Stock, Frederick, 45
Stockhausen, Karlheinz, 96
Stokowski, Leopold, 26, 45
Storm, Theodore, 'Schliesse mir die Augen beide', 13
Strauss, Richard, 4, 16; *Elektra*, 4
Stravinsky, Igor, 1, 2–3, 4, 6, 8, 9, 11, 13, 93
works: *Agon*, 101; *Apollo*, 4; Concerto for piano and wind instruments, 2; Concerto for two solo pianos, 3; Concerto in D for violin and orchestra, 1, 3, 4, 8; Concerto in E♭ ('Dumbarton Oaks'), 3, 4; *Jeu de Cartes*, 4; Octet, 3; Serenade in A, 3, 4; Sonata, 3; *Symphonies of Wind Instruments*, 3; Symphony in C, 3, 4; *Symphony of Psalms*, 3, 4
Strickland, William, 46
Suk, Josef, 46
Szeryng, Henryk, 46
Szigeti, Joseph, 45, 94
Szymanowski, Karol, Violin Concerto No. 2, Op. 61, 5

Tchaikovsky, Pyotr, Violin Concerto in D, Op. 35, 35
Thomson, Virgil, 94

120